CW00821287

Point of View in Fiction

A BUSY WRITER'S GUIDE

Marcy Kennedy

Tongue Untied Communications
ONTARIO, CANADA

Marcy Kennedy
marcykennedy@gmail.com
www.marcykennedy.com

Book Layout ©2013 BookDesignTemplates.com
Edited by Chris J. Saylor
Cover Design by Melinda VanLone

Point of View in Fiction/ Marcy Kennedy —1st ed.
ISBN 978-1-988069-03-6

Contents

i

Why a Busy Writer's Guide?

EVERY LIST ABOUT HOW TO BECOME A better writer includes studying craft. Years ago, as a new writer, I took that advice to heart but found that many craft books didn't give me the detailed, in-the-trenches coverage of a topic I needed. They included a lot of beautifully written prose and theory without explaining how to practically apply the principles, or they gave numerous examples but didn't explain how to replicate those concepts in my own work.

I ended up buying three or four books on the same topic to understand it and get the balance of theory and practice I was looking for. I spent more time studying craft than writing, and all the exercises in the books seemed to take me away from my story rather than helping me work directly on it. For the modern writer who also needs to blog and be on social media, who might be juggling a day job, and who still wants time to see their family or friends, that's a problem. Do you know anyone who doesn't have more commitments than they're able to handle already without adding "study the writing craft" on top of it?

We're busy. We're tired. We're overworked. We love writing, but often wonder if it's worth the sacrifices we're making for it. We know we're headed down the fast track to burning out, but don't know what we can do differently.

To quote *Allan F. Mogensen,* the creator of "Work Simplification," it's time to work smarter, not harder.

I wrote *The Busy Writer's Guide* series to help you fast-track the learning process. I felt that writers needed a fluff-free guide that would give them the detailed coverage of a topic they required while also respecting their time. I want you to be able to spend the majority of your writing time actually writing, so that you can set aside your computer and enjoy the people and experiences that make life worth living.

Each *Busy Writer's Guide* is intended to serve as an accelerated master's class in a topic. I'll give you enough theory so that you can understand why things work and why they don't, and enough examples to see how that theory looks in practice. I'll also provide tips and exercises to help you take it to the pages of your own story with an editor's-eye view.

My goal is for you to come away a stronger writer, with a stronger piece of work, than when you came in.

How Is This Guide Different From the Others?

Before we get started, I want to mention how this *Busy Writer's Guide* differs from the other *Busy Writer's Guides.* You might have already noticed that it's a touch longer. It's longer because point of view is about picking the "person" of your story (first, second, third, or omniscient), but it's also about maintaining consistency once you've picked your point of view. I considered splitting it into two books, but it didn't feel right to me to ask you to buy two books if you wanted all the material.

(I will have a separate book coming out in late 2015/early 2016 on deep POV, however, since that's an advanced technique that required a book to itself to truly do it justice.)

So, instead of giving you two books on point of view in general, I'll explain how this book is structured, allowing you to use it in the way that best suits your needs.

The first part of the book explains your point of view options, the common problems with those points of view, and tips for making the most of the one you choose. The second part of the book digs in to deal with avoiding point-of-view errors, choosing the right number of point-of-view characters for your story, and so on.

Ideally, to understand this topic completely, you'd read it all. You'll write better in your chosen point of view when you also understand the other points of view and how they're different from yours.

If you're really pressed for time, though, you have the option of reading only the chapters from the first part that define point of view and cover the point of view you're interested in, and then skipping to Chapter Seven, where I move into discussing point-of-view errors, starting with head-hopping.

Now that you know your options, let's get started.

CHAPTER ONE

Defining Point of View in Fiction

ONE OF THE MOST COMMON PROBLEMS I
see in the projects I edit is errors in point of view. That's
partly because point of view is closely connected to showing vs. telling and internal dialogue. It's also partly because it's a mul-
ti-faceted topic.

As I try to do in all my *Busy Writer's Guides*, I'm going to break
the topic down for you and walk you through it so that you come
away with a strong enough grasp on point of view to consistently
apply it in your fiction.

To start, we need to talk a little bit about point of view (POV) in
general. What is it? Why does it matter that we get it "right"?

> **Definition:** Point of view is a position or perspective from
> which something is considered or evaluated; a standpoint
> (Merriam-Webster Dictionary).

When we talk about point of view in fiction, we basically mean the perspective from which the story is told. Who are we listening to when we read the story? Whose head are we in? Whose opinions and judgments on events are we hearing? In a practical sense, POV lays the foundation for everything we'll write in our story.

WHAT DOES A CLEAR POINT OF VIEW DO FOR OUR STORIES?

Point of view errors cause many problems within fiction. They can leave the reader feeling whiplashed from one character to another, never giving them time to properly connect with and care about any one character. They can cause confusion and break the fictional dream as the reader struggles to figure out whose point of view they're in. And much more.

But I wanted to come at this from a different angle and talk about what a strong, clear, consistent point of view can do for our stories.

A clear point of view allows the reader to experience (and participate in) a situation that they could never have been part of, or might never want to be part of, in real life. Consistent and skilled use of POV not only allows us to live vicariously, but also gives us the opportunity to examine ourselves and think about whether we would have made the same choices as the characters. In other words, we become participants in two senses of the word. It engages our emotions and our minds.

A clear point of view builds subtext, as we're able to contrast what's happening around the character with what they think about it. We can sort through the difference between reality and perception, the difference between the objective and subjective.

A clear point of view sets each character apart, as we see how they uniquely interpret the world around them. Research has shown that avid readers are more empathetic in their real lives because reading opens them up to seeing the world from a perspective that might be very different from their own. As novelists and short story writers, we have a unique advantage in that we can give our audience that filtered perspective. They can't receive that from television or movies or plays.

A clear point of view controls the flow of information to either create suspense or forward the plot. As authors, how we choose to handle POV determines what we must and can't show to the reader. As readers, it creates the page-turning excitement as we discover things along with the POV character.

A clear point of view encourages showing rather than telling. "Showing" in fiction rather than "telling" is one of the most common pieces of writing advice and also one that a majority of writers struggle to execute. Understanding and writing from a close point of view makes this concept easier because we're experiencing the story through the eyes of a particular character.

A clear point of view helps us decide what description belongs in the story. Many writers buy into the fallacy that description slows a story down. Description doesn't slow a story down—bad description or description placed where it doesn't belong slows a story down. When we write with a clear point of view, we'll know what details are important to include and when is the appropriate time to include them.

A clear point of view shows us when to include backstory and when to explain details about our world and setting or about the way something works. How much or how little to explain these elements to readers becomes a stumbling block for many writers. When we have a clear POV, we'll know to include it only when the POV character would naturally be thinking about it or noticing it.

So now that you know some of the reasons a clear point of view matters, I want to define point of view in more depth. The better we understand it, the better we'll be able to execute it.

THE MULTIPLE LAYERS OF POINT OF VIEW

Much of the confusion around POV arises from the fact that we have multiple facets to point of view. We have the four "persons": first person, second person, limited third person, and omniscient. Within limited third person, our point of view can take on different levels of narrative distance, with the closest being what's called intimate or deep POV.

Then, to add to that, on a scene-by-scene level, we can have different point-of-view characters (what I'll be calling viewpoint characters from now on to help ease some of the term confusion).

As I mentioned in the introduction, in the first half of this book, I'm going to explain the four different points of view you can choose from when writing your story—the first person, second person, limited third person, and omniscient mentioned above. As I go through them, I'm going to outline the strengths and weaknesses of each option so that you'll be better prepared to decide which is the best option for your book.

As we talk about each type, I'm also going to look at what this means for us on a practical level—how to avoid the major problems that come with writing in that point of view and how to stay consistent to that point of view.

Once we've looked at the four different points of view, in the remainder of the book, I'll cover some of the most common point of view problems and questions, starting with head-hopping and other point-of-view errors. Although head-hopping is the most commonly discussed point-of-view error, it's not the only one, nor is it actually the most common.

From there, I'll be moving on to understanding the difference between narrative distance and author intrusion. I'll finish with how to choose a viewpoint character and tips for juggling multiple viewpoint characters.

I'm going to start with the least common point of view option—second person point of view.

Second-Person Point of View

SECOND-PERSON POINT OF VIEW USES *YOU* in the story rather than *he* or *she*.

So that you can get a feel for it, I'm going to show you an example.

You know how this looks to the folks in suits walking by on their way to work. You're leaning over a dumpster, your clothes mud-smeared and smelling of old fish. But you're willing to let them think whatever they want. Last thing you need is extra attention, and people ignore the homeless 'cause they don't want to be asked for money.

The sickly sweet smell of rotting fruit blocks your throat. You choke back your gag reflex and dig deeper into the trash. The tracking device stashed in your pocket says this is the place. Somewhere in among the dirty diapers, three-day old carrot peels, and soda cans some jerk should have recycled hides the briefcase that will change your fortune.

Very few successful books have been written in second-person point of view, but examples include *Bright Lights, Big City* by Jay McInerney and *If On A Winter's Night a Traveler* by Italo Calvino.

Second person is the only POV that I'm going to advise you again using, unless you're writing a Choose Your Own Adventure-style story. If you're writing a CYOA-style story (and they are coming back into some popularity thanks to ebooks and apps), then you must use second person. Otherwise, I strongly advise you against it.

And here's why:

The theoretical advantage to using second-person POV is that it places the reader as a character in the story, and they should feel more engaged and involved. Right?

Notice that I said *theoretical* advantage. In actual execution, it tends to distance the reader from the story because they're constantly aware that they're not actually doing the things the story says they are. It also has the biggest problem with gender cross-over of any of the POVs. *Bright Lights, Big City* is a great example. I'm a woman, but the "you" in that story is a man. So the "you" obviously isn't me, which makes it awkward.

You could self-publish a regular novel in second-person POV, but your chances of traditionally publishing a book written in second person are slim.

I'm going to talk a little more about where you can find resources if you'd like to write a CYOA-style story, and then we won't talk about second person again in this book. Once we're out of this chapter, we're going to talk exclusively about the three popular and accepted POVs—first person, limited third person, and omniscient.

CHOOSE YOUR OWN ADVENTURE-STYLE STORIES

In case you've never heard of a CYOA-style story before, they're basically a system where the reader is the protagonist and, at various points, they're able to make a decision that affects the course of the story. If you're going to write one of these stories, however, be careful about actually calling it that since the term "choose your own adventure" is trademarked.

Along with being written in second person, these types of stories are also usually written in present tense (as you may have noticed from my example above). Some readers love present tense, some hate it, and some will only tolerate it if the book offers them enough of an inducement to temporarily overlook it (such as did *The Hunger Games* and *The Help*). Writing in present tense is extremely difficult to do well, so if you don't love this tense to begin with, CYOA-style writing might not be for you.

If you're still interested in trying it, here are some resources that can help.

Programs to Help You Build Your Decision Tree

If you're someone who hates plotting out a story in advance, CYOA-style projects probably aren't for you for that reason, either. To keep the multiple potential storyline directions straight, CYOA-style stories require what's called a *decision tree*. (If you'd like to see an example, you can look at the image of the decision tree for *Edward Packard's The Mystery of Chimney Rock*, published by Bantam Books, online.)

You can use paper for this process, but there are also now various programs available to help. Some of them will even allow you to write the story inside of them and export it.

Since I don't currently write CYOA-style stories, I haven't tried these programs myself, but this shortlist was recommended by writers who do.

Twinery (http://twinery.org/) - An online resource that allows you to write online and export what you create as an HTML.

SimpleMind+ (http://www.simpleapps.eu/simplemind/) - A mind-mapping tool for iPad or iPhone that you can use to create your decision tree.

Inklewriter (http://www.inklestudios.com/inklewriter/) - This software is free to use, but they currently charge a small export fee if you want your story turned into a downloadable HTML document or converted into an Amazon-ready file. They provide sample files so you can see what your file would look like after either service.

Website Articles About CYOA-Style Writing

Since this isn't a book about writing a CYOA-style story, I can't go into detail on all the things you need to consider and do for this unique literature form. What I can do is direct you to some fantastic further reading on the topic. You can find these articles by typing the titles into your Internet browser's search bar.

5 Rules for Writing Interesting Choices in Multiple Choice Games – Don't let the title deceive you. Even though this post is technically about designing a game, his advice applies equally well the writing a CYOA-style story, which is basically just a text-based game.

One Book, Many Readings – Be forewarned. This site is white text on a black background and it's long—you will see spots afterward. That said, this is a very in-depth exploration of CYOA-style stories vs. the more linear format.

How to Write Choose Your Own Adventure – Karen Woodward succinctly covers the important elements of a CYOA-style story, including what to add into each story block, selecting your story endings and secondary characters, and the value of sub-plots.

Online Examples

Some authors are exploring variations on the CYOA-style style through interactive storytelling on their blogs as a way to connect with readers.

Jen Kirchner, author of *The Fourth Channel*, created a series of blog posts where readers voted for the decision that would direct the story. Kirchner took the most popular selection and wrote the next installment based on that choice. You can read *The Cure* on her website.

Amber West, author of *The Ruth Valley Missing*, also wrote what she called an interactive web serial. You can read all the installments and see how she allowed readers to direct the story from her website A Day Without Sushi.

> **Want easy access to the resources mentioned in this book? Go to www.marcykennedy.com/pointofview and enter the password** perspective.

CHAPTER THREE

Omniscient Point of View

OMNISCIENT POV IS WHEN THE STORY IS told by an all-knowing narrator who is not a character in the story.

That all-knowing narrator is (normally) the author, and the story is told in his or her voice rather than in any particular character's voice. (I'll talk about an exception to the author-as-narrator guideline at the end of this chapter.)

> **Definition:** Omniscience is having infinite awareness, understanding, and insight; being possessed of universal or complete knowledge (Merriam-Webster Dictionary).

The omniscient narrator can tell the reader what any of the characters is thinking or feeling. They can describe things that none of the characters know about. Consequently, omniscient POV is easily confused with head-hopping. Head-hopping and omniscient POV are not the same thing. I'll explain the difference later, but you need to understand all the POVs before we can talk about what head-hopping is and what it isn't.

What's important to keep in mind for the moment is that omniscient POV is different from having multiple viewpoint characters. In omniscient POV, you only have one point of view (or viewpoint) and it's that of the omniscient narrator. The reader hears only one voice—that of the omniscient narrator.

The added distance from the characters means that omniscient POV often feels more formal and tends to share a similar tone with fables or parables. This difference in tone is created in part because omniscient POV includes more statements of fact and fewer statements that feel like personal opinions or judgments. When the omniscient narrator tells the reader that something is so (whether it's something about a character or something about the world in which the story takes place), it's the truth. You don't have the same room for interpretation and subterfuge that you do in the closer points of view where the characters could be prejudiced, wrong, or lying to themselves.

I'm going to give you a couple examples of omniscient POV so that I can point out the hallmarks of this point of view type.

For our first example, let's say we have outlaws who kidnapped a marshal during the execution of a bank robbery. Now they're on the run, and have hired a guide to show them a little-known pathway to the Mexican border.

> Bonnie sauntered along behind their guide, hauling **the marshal like a horse by his tied hands and lassoed neck. Clyde trailed them at the end of the line, his gaze shifting from side to side, fingers twitching over his gun holster.**

"You made a huge mistake," Marshal Dillon said, *trying to keep a smidgen of his dignity as he staggered after Bonnie.* "My men'll never stop hunting you now. They'll block every path to the border and be waitin' in every town."

Bonnie's step gained a new bounce. "Every path they know."

Dillon scowled at her back.

I've highlighted a couple of things, but the first thing I want you to notice is the tone of it. We feel like we're watching this happen from a distance rather than being in any one character's head. That's one of the first clues that this might be omniscient. Omniscient POV feels like we're on the outside.

Another sign is the contrast between the passage I've bolded and the passage I've put in italics and underlined. In the bold passage, we're hearing about the marshal from the outside. Dillon wouldn't be thinking about himself as "the marshal" or that he was being led "like a horse." This sounds like we're watching from above. If we were in Dillon's POV, we'd be feeling the rope on our wrists and neck and there'd be fire in our veins at the way we were being treated. We also wouldn't see Clyde trailing behind us with an itchy trigger finger.

But then in the next paragraph, the narrator is able to tell us that Dillon is trying to keep some of his dignity and that he scowled at Bonnie's back. Bonnie isn't our narrator because she couldn't know these things.

There is absolutely no indication within this passage that we're tied to a particular character as the narrator. The narrator is outside of it all. The narrator knows everything, but isn't taking part in it.

Another hallmark of omniscient POV is when you have an analysis of a situation show up that doesn't belong to any of the characters. It comes from an outside source. Here's an example so you can see how this might look.

> "My wife'll do it," Henry said, jerking a thumb in Marge's direction. "She needs something useful to fill her time when the kids are at school since she doesn't have a job."
>
> **Henry often spoke about Marge like she wasn't there—or, more accurately, as though she were something not intelligent enough to know what he was saying about her, like a dog or a cat.**

The part in bold is the opinion of someone looking from on high. It doesn't belong to Henry because he doesn't see anything wrong with the way he talks about his wife. It doesn't belong to Marge because there's no sense of how she feels about Henry's treatment of her.

Examples of omniscient POV include Earnest Hemingway's *The Old Man and the Sea*, *Heist Society* by Ally Carter, *A Little Princess* by Frances Hodgson Burnett, Rachel Aaron's *The Legend of Eli Monpress* series, and J. K. Rowling's *Harry Potter* books.

WHAT ARE THE ADVANTAGES OF OMNISCIENT POV?

The biggest advantage of omniscient POV is that we're not constrained by what any single character knows at any single point in time. We can tell the reader things that the characters aren't aware of or wouldn't notice. This means that omniscient POV stories enable us to tell stories that can't be told well—or at all—through the limited perspectives of our characters.

In some stories, we might even want the emotional distance created by an omniscient narrator.

We're also able to let our authorial voice shine through without having to worry about trying to create a distinct and unique character voice for each viewpoint character because we don't have viewpoint characters.

WHAT ARE THE DISADVANTAGES OF OMNISCIENT POV?

Despite those seeming advantages, omniscient POV is extremely difficult to do well.

We have to engage the reader without the benefit of connection with a particular character, and we have to make our characters interesting from a distance.

We have to ensure that we're not accidentally head-hopping rather than using omniscient POV.

We have to make decisions about what to include without the help of a filtering character viewpoint. Omniscient means "all-knowing," not "all-telling." Just because we're writing in omniscient POV doesn't mean we give every possible detail. We still only give the details that are pertinent to the story, that enhance it in some way. This is more difficult to decide on in omniscient POV than in the closer POVs because, in a closer POV, what we show is what's important to the character at that moment in time. Consequently, omniscient POV stories are more at risk for passages of purple prose.

We also have a bigger challenge in trying not to lose sight of what the characters want within the context of the story. We might be the omniscient narrator, but our characters aren't mindless puppets. They still need strong reasons to act within the environment of their world. In omniscient POV, there's a greater risk of the author having a character act in a certain way because the story needs them to rather than because that action would naturally arise from the motivations, goals, and personalities of the characters themselves. When that happens, we lose believability. The reader doesn't feel like the characters are real people anymore. We've broken the fictional dream.

And, despite the success of the *Harry Potter* series, omniscient POV has largely fallen out of favor with modern readers.

Let me explain it this way.

When we're young, our mothers or fathers or grandparents tell us stories. They'll tell us what each character is thinking or feeling at any moment. They'll even tell us things the characters don't yet know. They're all-knowing in the story world.

And we're alright with that because we don't want to experience the story as if we were one of the characters. We want to safely watch from a distance while our loved one gives us the big-picture view.

Omniscient POV was also the default in most fiction 100 years ago. It would have been improper somehow to poke intimately into a stranger's story, and we weren't that far removed from the days when most people were illiterate and the majority of stories were still told orally.

But as we grow and as our society changed, we no longer want to be told a story. We want to see it and live it. We gobble up reality TV. We watch movies in 3D. Our video games are using cameras to capture our movements to power avatars we created to look like us. We now want stories written in first-person or in intimate third-person (deep POV). We want to feel like we're part of the story.

Because of the way our culture is, a story written in omniscient POV is a much harder sell than is a story written in one of the more intimate POVs. Harder but not impossible. Despite what I said above, not everyone wants to feel like they're a part of the story. Because of that, I don't think omniscient POV will ever truly die out.

KEY TO WRITING SUCCESSFULLY IN OMNISCIENT POV

If we're thinking about writing in omniscient POV, there are three criteria we need to meet to make it work.

#1 - We need a story that can't be told any other way.

I like to use Rachel Aaron's *Legend of Eli Monpress* books as the perfect example of this. I wouldn't have wanted her to write her books in third person because of what she would have lost.

She created a world where everything—even inanimate items—have a "spirit" in them. In *The Legend of Eli Monpress*, we're allowed to peek into the mind of a door, a regular rat, and many other creatures and objects you wouldn't normally be able to have as viewpoint characters. These creatures and objects aren't prominent characters, and so in a third-person limited POV, we'd never be able to hear from them, but hearing from them is part of what makes her books so fascinating.

To give us the full experience of her world and stories, she had to write in omniscient POV. Her stories couldn't have been fully told in any other way.

#2 - We need a strong, unique voice.

Voice is a little hard to define, but basically what we're talking about when we talk about a writer's voice is the distinctive way they string words together.

What types of imagery do they gravitate toward?

Is their writing serious? Quirky? Snarky? Funny?

What type of rhythm or cadence do they naturally use?

Are their sentences long and flowing or short and sharp?

How much dialogue do they use?

What word choices do they make?

Is their work dark or light-hearted?

Every choice we make, from the profanity level in our work to the amount and level of description, contributes to our voice. If you pull three different authors off your bookshelf and read the first chapter of their book, you should be able to recognize their individual voices. If I then showed you another passage from one of those writers and made you guess who it was from, if they have a strong voice, you should be able to identify the author.

In other POVs, our readers need to connect with and care about our viewpoint character(s). The story is told in their voice(s). Our voice is there, but it's less prominent. In omniscient POV, the reader needs to invest in us, the author, and our way of saying things. Our voice is the only voice. They continue reading because they want to hear how we, in particular, tell the story.

This is one of the main reasons why newer writers shouldn't usually start out their writing career by attempting omniscient POV. Voice takes time to develop.

And some writers never develop a strong, distinctive voice. That doesn't mean they can't write good books. It does mean they shouldn't write in omniscient POV.

Because this is such an important element of omniscient POV, I'm going to spend the next chapter giving you some tips for developing your voice (and they'll help you as a writer even if you don't plan on writing in omniscient POV).

#3 - We need to know the difference between omniscient POV and head-hopping.

Being able to distinguish between these two is the crux of writing in omniscient POV. Chapter Seven will be about understanding the difference between the two.

EXCEPTIONS TO THE OMNISCIENT AUTHOR-NARRATOR

In understanding omniscient POV well enough to write in it, it's important to address how far this point of view choice can stretch before it stops being omniscient POV and moves into either distant limited third person or a cool-toned first person.

At the start of this chapter, I said the all-knowing narrator of omniscient POV is *normally* the author. It's not always. Omniscient POV can stretch to include a non-authorial narrator.

To put this another way, we can have an omniscient narrator who is also a character created by the author—they're just not a character within the story. An excellent example of this is Death in Markus Zusak's *The Book Thief.* Death knows everything, and has a distinctive voice and unique perspective on the story, but isn't a part of it. If you take a look at this example, you'll also notice that this means omniscient POV can be written in first person. It's not confined to third person.

Opportunities to create these types of unusual omniscient stories are rare, however, because true omniscience isn't a quality many possess, and to qualify as omniscient POV, the narrator needs to be standing apart from the story in some way, able to observe it all. In other words, they almost need to be omnipresent as well.

I've seen confusion arise over omniscient POV when someone forgets those defining characteristics. It's easy to confuse a well-informed character narrator with an omniscient narrator. A well-informed character within a story may know almost everything, but they're still not omniscient.

As an example, an often confused book is Julian Fellowes' *Snobs*. The narrator knows almost everything because he has the perspective of hindsight and because he's the close and trusted confidant of the other characters in the story. But calling this omniscient POV shows a fundamental misunderstanding of what makes a story omniscient. Not only is the narrator in *Snobs* a part of the story himself, but he's also not all-knowing—as he admits in the very first line of the book.

It might seem like I'm being hard-nosed about this, but good writing isn't forwarded by perpetuating fallacies. All an unclear understanding of something does is confuse more writers. To write any of the points of view well, we need to know what they *are* and what they *aren't*.

CHAPTER FOUR

Tips for Developing Your Voice

I'VE ALREADY SAID THIS, BUT I'M GOING TO say it again so that there's no chance of anyone misunderstanding. No matter what point of view we choose to write in, it's important to develop our personal voice as a writer.

I'm focusing on it after talking about omniscient point of view because a distinctive writing voice happens to play a special role when writing in omniscient POV. We can't write a good omniscient story without a strong voice.

> **Definition of Voice:** An instrument or medium of expression (Merriam-Webster Dictionary).

Regardless of the POV we're writing in, a distinct voice seems to be the thing that everyone wants but no one can tell you how to get. And I have to admit that this annoys me. I'm a practical person. If you can tell me how to do something, I'll get it done for you. If it's ooey gooey and you tell me "it just has to develop over time," I'm going to be cheesed. And then I'm going to try to find a way to efficiently develop and teach that thing.

I believe that developing your voice—like everything else in writing—takes time and discipline, but it can be done. So here are some ways you can actively work on developing your voice.

Learn the Basics of Writing

Before you argue that this will only teach you to write like everyone else, hear me out.

Can an artist sculpt a lifelike statue without first learning about the properties of different types of stone and without learning how to use a chisel and other tools? Can a pianist compose a sonata without first learning which notes sound good together? Can they pass that music along to others without first learning how to write those notes down on sheet music?

Monet, Van Gogh, and Picasso are all considered innovators in the art world, but they still used the same surfaces, had to learn the same techniques and brush strokes, and blended paints in the same way as every other artist. They didn't innovate in the craft. They innovated in what they created through the craft.

One of the most important things a writer trying to develop their voice can do is to read craft books. Writing is just like any other skill, whether that be painting, woodworking, engineering, or neurosurgery. We have to be so solid on the basics that they come instinctively before we're truly able to create something fresh and unique.

POINT OF VIEW | 29

Set Boundaries

In her excellent post on "Ways to Develop Your Unique Writing Voice," social media maven and bestselling author Kristen Lamb pointed out how boundaries can actually free your creativity rather than limit you. She likened setting boundaries in writing to narrowing down what means of transportation you want to use to take your vacation. Your spontaneity and creativity in your vacation aren't destroyed simply because you chose to travel by car rather than by boat. But it does help you narrow down the kinds of adventures you're going to have. And that's not a bad thing. If you don't at least start with some broad guidelines like how you plan to travel, you'll never get anywhere at all.

Likewise, if you want to develop your voice more quickly, pick a point of view and a genre and stick to it until you've mastered it.

How will this help? Each genre comes with conventions that you need to follow to write in it. POV adds structure and establishes how you can tell your story. When some of these big decisions are settled, you're free to focus on the actual writing. In other words, you're free to allow your voice to come out.

Read and Analyze

Read a lot is one of the few pieces of advice novelists are given for developing their voice. But reading alone isn't enough. You need to figure out what works in these books and what doesn't. What do you love and hate about them? It could be something big picture (like the way they weave their theme throughout the book) or it could be something more subtle (like the cadence they use in their sentences).

For each book you read, try to identify and write down three things you loved and three things you didn't. For the things that you didn't enjoy about the book, ask yourself why you didn't like them and how you would have done them differently.

What you love and hate helps you define what you want to be and what you don't, as well as what you're naturally drawn to. Chances are good that, if you're not writing in a way that you would love to read, you're not being authentic either.

Make a List of Words That Describe Your Personality

In her post about "Author Voice Vs. Character Voice," erotic romance writer Roni Loren describes her author voice and then points out how it directly relates to who she is as a person and how she approaches life. Your voice is you.

Sit down and make a list of 15-20 words that describe you, then elaborate on each and how you see that trait expressed in a normal day.

For example, I'm quirky, sarcastic, thoughtful, and structured, and I see the dark in the world but fight for the light. So is my voice. By identifying who I am, I can look at my writing and see what parts are true to me and what parts aren't.

Stop Reading Novels

I know. I know. Up above, I told you to read and analyze. That was one step along the path. But eventually, you're going to need to make sure that you're starting to sound like you rather than subconsciously copying another writer. The only sure way to do that is to stop reading other people's work.

Take one to two months and use your reading time to write instead (or exchange novels for books on craft).

This isn't meant to be maintained long-term. You only need to stay in this stage until you start hearing yourself. I made the biggest jump in developing my own voice when I stopped reading temporarily.

Read Your Work Out Loud

What flows off your tongue? What comes naturally? What doesn't?

Reading your work out loud helps you smooth out the tongue-twister passages and create more realistic dialogue, but it also helps with voice. What sounds right to your ear? Could you see telling the story this way out loud to your friends?

Blog to Get Comfortable Being You in Public

In a post she wrote a few years ago, YA author Susan Bischoff said that one of the benefits she gained from blogging was that "I learned how to be myself. In public. I don't think that's something that comes naturally to most people."

The only way you can develop your unique voice is to be proud of who you are and how you sound. As soon as you start worrying about what other people will think or whether they'll like your voice, you're going to start trying to change it.

Blogging helps you learn to be comfortable with who you are and with sharing who you are with readers. Writing magazine articles is another way to help develop your voice in a public forum, as is public speaking through a group like Toast Masters. If you're fine with giving your work away for free, you could also try posting your writing on a platform like Wattpad.

AUTHOR VOICE VS. CHARACTER VOICE

Some of you might be confused or concerned because I said that, in closer POVs, character voice will supplant authorial voice.

For those of us who plan to write in a closer POV, what does this mean for us in terms of voice?

Many elements of voice—such as how much dialogue we use and the overall tone of our stories—isn't affected by the POV we're writing in. Those are big-picture choices. And that's where our voice will still come through regardless—in the big-picture elements.

If you're writing romance, the level of heat you include and how you describe intimate moments between characters is part of your brand and part of your voice. It's something readers come to expect from you and come to enjoy about your writing.

If you choose to write stories with sad endings—a la Nicholas Sparks—then that's part of your style, part of the expectation readers carry with them when they come to your writing.

How you end up integrating theme into your stories is part of your voice. Different writers integrate theme in different ways, with varying levels of obviousness and subtlety.

So even when our characters take over the voice on the page and the word choices, judgments, and cadence become theirs, our voice is still there, hidden in the big-picture choices we've made.

CHAPTER FIVE

First-Person Point of View

IN FIRST-PERSON POINT OF VIEW, THE narrator is a character within the story. They use pronouns like *I, me, we, us, mine,* and *ours.* Just like it sounds, in first person, the character is telling us the story directly.

> I dug through my purse. No keys. They were here yester-
> day. I'd dropped them in when I came home from work,
> didn't I? I tipped my purse's contents out onto the table,
> and receipts, old gum wrappers, and pennies spilled every-
> where.

We have to make a few choices about our first-person POV story right off the bat.

Choice #1 – How Many Narrators?

So that no one stumbles over terminology here, when we're talking about narrators in first-person POV, we're talking about viewpoint characters. How many viewpoint characters are we going to have?

Most of the time, when we use first-person POV, we'll only use that single viewpoint character throughout the book (like in *The Hunger Games* by Suzanne Collins or *The Shifter* by Janice Hardy). However, that's not a rule. Authors have successfully used more than one first-person narrator in the same book or have used a combination of first and third.

We can use multiple first-person narrators like in Kathryn Stockett's *The Help* or Audrey Niffenegger's *The Time Traveler's Wife*. However, I wouldn't recommend using multiple first-person narrators for new writers because it's difficult to do well.

When we have multiple first-person narrators in a book, we need to use some external means of signaling to the reader that we've switched narrators. So, for example, we might label each chapter or scene with the narrator's name the way Kathryn Stockett did in *The Help* and the way Fabio Bueno did in *Wicked Sense*.

We can use a single first-person narrator for most of the story and then switch to third person for scenes where the first-person narrator isn't present. The theory behind this is that the first-person narrator is telling us the story, and the parts in third person are pieces he was told about later. An example of this is *Dragon Bones* by Patricia Briggs. This only works, however, if you're writing in past tense. (I'll talk about that choice in a minute.)

We can use first person for the villain's scenes in an otherwise third-person POV book. This is a way we can hide the identity of the villain. (After all, how many of us think of our names on a regular basis? I don't.) Julie Garwood did this in her romance novel *The Bride*.

We can use third and first to set apart a time gap between the different viewpoint characters. For example, in Kathleen Duey's *Skin*

Hunger, the two viewpoint characters are separated by 500 years. Duey uses first-person POV for the character who is in the present day and third-person POV for the character who is in the past.

Or, if we just want to dip our toes into first person, we can use it as a bookend prologue and epilogue to an otherwise third-person POV story like in Beverly Lewis' *The Shunning*.

Because we now have all these options, in at least some cases, it eliminates one of the major disadvantages of first person, which was that we needed to tell the entire story from one single person's viewpoint.

If we decide to use more than one viewpoint character in a first-person story, though, we need to be careful that we're making the choice for the right reasons. We'll talk about this more later when we look at choosing the right number of viewpoint characters and further considerations for selecting our point of view.

Choice #2 – Present Tense vs. Past Tense

One of the advantages of first-person POV is how well it works with present tense. In omniscient and third person, using present tense can feel artificial, but in first person, it comes across like we're simply eavesdropping into the mind of the character thinking to herself.

I'll give you an example of a passage written in both tenses so you can see the difference. Past tense first.

> The avalanche's roar stopped, and I opened my eyes. Or thought I did. The ice cave where I'd taken shelter was solid black.
>
> I pulled my pack off my back and fished around the outside for my flashlight. There. Still there. It hadn't broken off in my mad dash or when I crammed myself through the crack in the ice wall. I pushed the *on* button without unclipping it from my pack.

Light flooded the cave and bounced off the walls, setting off a sequence of glitters. The once-translucent ceiling
that let in colors from the outside world before the avalanche was now a solid gray. A white wall plugged the entrance crack, and a cascade of snow spilled two feet in.

I scuttled to the blocked entrance. "Help!"

My scream seemed to crumple back in on me, like talking underwater. Even if my team had survived the avalanche, would they be able to hear me? I gulped in a breath,
but it didn't satisfy. Without rescue, it'd be a toss-up which
would kill me first—starvation, hypothermia, or running
out of air.

Written in present tense, this same passage would have sounded
like this...

The avalanche's roar stops, and I open my eyes. At least
I think I did. The ice cave where I've taken shelter is solid
black.

I pull my pack off my back and fish around the outside
for my flashlight. There. Still there. It hasn't broken off in
my mad dash or when I crammed myself through the crack
in the ice wall. I push the *on* button without unclipping it
from my pack.

Light floods the cave and bounces off the walls, setting
off a sequence of glitters. The once-translucent ceiling that
let in colors from the outside world before the avalanche is
now a solid gray. A white wall plugs the entrance crack,
and a cascade of snow spills two feet in.

I scuttle to the blocked entrance. "Help!"

My scream seems to crumple back in on me, like talking
underwater. Even if my team has survived the avalanche,
will they be able to hear me? But they might all be dead,
and if they are, no rescue's coming.

I gulp in a breath, but it doesn't satisfy. Without rescue,
it'll be a toss-up which kills me first—starvation, hypothermia, or running out of air.

Present tense is growing in popularity. So this isn't a right or wrong. This is a choose-what-feels-right-for-your-story situation.

To help you decide, I'll walk through how past vs. present tense influences our first-person story.

In first person present tense, the character is relating the story as it happens to them. They have no more knowledge than the reader does of how things will turn out.

Many authors who choose to use present tense in first person do so because it eliminates a common first-person narrator "problem" in past tense. In first person past tense, the reader knows that, technically, the narrator can't die. Some people believe this removes part of the tension in a story where the reader would otherwise worry about the narrator's life. While there are other ways around that dilemma (as we'll see in a moment), many of them end up feeling artificial. By writing in present tense, the theory is that it reintroduces the tension because we're watching the story play out at the moment it's happening. Whether or not you agree that this reintroduces the tension is up to you to decide, but this is one of the supposed strengths of writing in present tense when you're also using first person.

Both *The Help* and *The Hunger Games* were written in first person present tense. They're also both stories where an important element of the story is the threat to the narrators' lives.

In first person past tense, the first-person narrator is telling the story retrospectively, reporting it to the reader at some point after the story has taken place.

Most first person past tense stories don't identify the *when* of this later date, but it adds an interesting element to the story when they do because what we give to the reader isn't just the story— it's the narrator's interpretation of the story and of their younger selves. They already know what's going to happen.

While it might sound like first-person point of view is the complete reverse of omniscient point of view, where the story is narrated by an external other, they're more like doppelgängers. They share one important element in common—when writing in first person past tense with an identified or implied *when*, both the first-person viewpoint character and the omniscient narrator are technically telling their story to someone. In this way, they're more like each other than either are like limited third-person POV. (We'll look at this a bit more when we talk about the reliability of our first-person narrator.)

To avoid the "first person narrator can't die" issue of past tense, some authors have placed the narrator in the afterlife, reflecting back on how they reached that point. As you might imagine, the dead narrator comes with its own problems. Even though your narrator might not have died during the events in the story, and might have lived a full life only to die in their sleep at the age of ninety, readers might assume they die during the story and be turned away by that foreknowledge.

In a story where the *when* isn't given, first person past tense is usually treated functionally just like third person past tense—the character is presumed to know only what's happening in the story's present and doesn't forecast about what's to come or talk about things they didn't know at the time.

The books in Janice Hardy's *The Healing Wars* series are good examples of first person past tense stories where it's treated as if the character has no knowledge of what's to come.

A less conventional option is also to mix past tense and present tense. For example, you might have a character who keeps a dairy.

If you're writing in first person, what I recommend is that you take just one scene and try it in both past tense and present tense. One or the other will probably feel more natural to you.

Choice #3 – Will Your Narrator Also Be the Protagonist?

The narrator is the person telling the story (in a first-person POV, it's the *I*).

The protagonist is the person the story is about. The protagonist is the one driving the plot, and it's their goal that the story focuses on.

Most of the time in a first-person POV story, our narrator and our protagonist will be the same person, but they don't have to be. The most famous example is *The Great Gatsby*, where Nick Carraway is our first-person narrator but Jay Gatsby is the protagonist. These stories are often called *first person observer* stories.

Even though the narrator will have their own goals, obstacles, and motivations, they're not the one driving the story. Instead, they're observing the protagonist and, in some sense, participating in the protagonist's quest. The focus of the story needs to stay on the protagonist.

We might want to write a first person observer story for one of the following reasons.

Reason #1 – Readers wouldn't enjoy being inside the head of our protagonist. First-person POV stories are extremely intimate. We're closely connected to the narrator, without a break, for the entire story (assuming we choose a single narrator). Not every character is someone readers would want to be that close to for that long. A good example is Sherlock Holmes. Holmes is too intelligent, too proud, too cold. Being in his mind for any length of time would become unbearable. Watching him through the eyes of the more normal Dr. Watson, however, makes him fascinating.

Reason #2 – It would be too difficult to write from the viewpoint of our protagonist or would cause the reader to have to work too hard to read the story. First-person POV stories require us to write in the voice of our narrator character. There is no distance. So a character who spends most of their time in a drug-induced state, has a severe mental disorder, or is illiterate or has a tough-to-parse dialect will create problems as a narrator. Some writers have experimented with this successfully, but those types of viewpoints are difficult to execute. A good example if you want to see it done is the novel *Flowers for Algernon* by Daniel Keyes. The book is written in the form of a journal belonging to Charlie Gordon. When the story opens, Charlie has an IQ of 68 and becomes a test subject for a surgery designed to enhance intelligence. Grammatical errors and spelling mistakes riddle the opening of the book, disappear as Charlie's intelligence rises to a peak of 185, and return again as the operation begins to fail.

Reason #3 – The story would be much less interesting from the protagonist's perspective because there would be no mystery (or withholding things would create reader anger). In Sir Arthur Conan Doyle's *Sherlock Holmes* mysteries, Holmes usually figures out the solution long before the rest of us. The mysteries would have been much less intriguing if we'd been in Holmes' perspective, where the solution was easily come to. We enjoy them more because we're struggling along with Watson to figure it out.

First-person narrators who aren't aware of the reader (so in present tense or in first-person past tense that's being functionally treated like a third-person POV) can't intentionally withhold anything. If they would think about it, if they know about it, it has to go onto the page.

If you check out the 1- and 2-star reviews on Amazon for *The Girl on the Train* by Paula Hawkins, you'll see why this is so important. Despite the popularity of this book, it has an unusually large number of unhappy reviews. Many of the complaints center around the fact that Meagan, one of three first-person narrators in the book, omits things from her own thoughts that should have been there.

This book is written in present tense, so there shouldn't be any withholding by the narrators. They don't know anyone is listening to their thoughts, so they'd have no reason to edit them. Yet Hawkins withheld things that Meagan would have normally been thinking in order to insert a twist at the end. Using Meagan as a viewpoint character created a huge problem even though she wasn't the protagonist. The problem would be magnified ten-fold had she been.

If you want to see an example of how an author used a first-person observer so as not to intentionally deceive the reader while also not revealing all the protagonist's secrets up front, take a look at John Irving's *A Prayer for Owen Meany*. Owen is the protagonist (who, you find out as the book goes on, believes he has a very special mission in life), but the narrator is Owen's friend, John Wheelwright.

Reason #4 – You want to kill off your protagonist. Earlier I pointed out that one of the problems with a first-person narrator is the issue of whether or not they can die. A possible solution to this is to have a non-narrator protagonist. Then your protagonist can die, while your narrator remains alive to tell the story.

THE KEY STRENGTH OF FIRST-PERSON POV

One of the major strengths of first-person POV is that it's easier to establish intimacy. We're being brought into the confidence of a character. Many readers enjoy first-person POV because they feel like they're sitting down with a friend who's telling them a story. This is especially true among young adult readers.

HOW TO IMPROVE YOUR FIRST-PERSON POV

This is the spot where we really dig into the practical application. What questions do we need to ask ourselves when we're writing first-person POV, what special challenges do we face, and how can we solve them?

Why is your first-person narrator telling this story?

This is a question you only need to ask yourself if you're writing in first person past tense and you're acknowledging that your first-person narrator is telling the story from some point in the future. In other words, you're treating this as a retrospective narrative rather than treating it as functionally the same as a third person past tense story.

By its very nature, this type of retrospective first-person point of view is more self-conscious than any of the other POVs. The POV character is telling their story to someone. You can see hints of this in the way many (though not all) first-person stories include a paragraph where the narrator introduces himself or points out directly that they're telling their story. Take a look at how the first-person narrator Elodie does it in Kait Nolan's YA novel *Red*.

I was thirteen when I found out why my mother left me.

It seems important to start my story there. The moment when my life changed and everything became a nightmare. The moment when my mother's madness began to infect my father. Infect me.

Elodie continues on to tell the reader that it's her seventeenth birthday, and she's gone out into the woods to consider killing herself because she's a werewolf.

You can also take a look at how Harry Dresden does this in Jim Butcher's *Storm Front*. Before the end of the first page, you'll find a paragraph where Harry Dresden gives the reader his full name, location, and profession—wizard.

These introductions are always going to come in Chapter One, and usually they happen right on the first page, sometimes in the first paragraph.

Because these first person past tense stories are stories that the narrator is telling to someone, they often feel like they need to introduce themselves.

We, as the writer, need to know why our first-person narrator is telling the story and who their intended audience is.

Why does this matter?

The purpose, intention, or goal of the first-person viewpoint character in telling the story is what should be driving our narrative. Everything we write should forward the goal the first-person narrator has in telling their story. By knowing this, we give our story focus it won't otherwise have.

We don't have to directly reveal your first-person narrator's goal or their intended audience to the reader. In most cases, we shouldn't directly reveal them. But they need to be clear in our heads.

Is your narrator reliable or unreliable?

Again, this only applies to a retrospective first-person story. If you're treating your story as functionally the same as a third person past tense, then you don't need to worry about this.

The self-conscious nature of the retrospective first-person POV story means the reader can't always be certain if the narrator is reliable or unreliable. Beyond this, the narrator can be either intentionally or unintentionally unreliable.

In limited third-person POV, the point-of-view character can lie to themselves, lie to other characters, or have a false impression of reality, but they can't lie to the reader because they're not aware the reader exists. Large parts of the story will be "objective" because they're "outside" the POV character. This is the biggest difference between first and third. In first person past tense, the character is talking to us in some sense. Because they're speaking to us, they can also lie to us.

Let me break down what I mean by that a little more.

If we're writing properly in third-person POV, everything is filtered through the eyes of the character. However, it's still just filtering. We still see what happens in an objective sense. The driver in front of our POV character slams on their breaks and our POV character hits them because she was tailgating. That's what objectively happened. How it's described and what details we receive depend on the POV character. She might not have realized she was driving so close until the accident happened. She might have known but thought she could stop in time. But it'll be clear that she was tailgating and that slamming into the car in front of her was accidental. It's like a coloring book where the POV character fills in the colors but the lines are already there.

In first person, however, it's not just filtered. It's created. They might tell us that they accidentally slammed into the car in front of them, but it might not have been an accident at all. They might be interpreting events for us in such a way as to make us believe that they weren't out to get their ex-husband's new wife. It's like having a blank page where the POV character first draws the picture and then colors it in.

Which means we have to ask, "Are they lying to us?" Presenting themselves in a certain way, even if it's not entirely accurate, because they want to be perceived in a particular way (for example, they want the reader's sympathy or respect)? Because they want to convince us of something? Are they unable to see reality, and so they're giving us their perception but not the truth, making them unintentionally unreliable? Playing with these aspects is part of the fun of using a first-person retrospective narrator and also part of the challenge.

Let me be clear. We don't need to write an unreliable narrator in a first-person story. But it is an option we have.

If we're writing an unreliable narrator, we'll need to drop subtle hints for the reader. The reader wants to be able to figure out what's really happening, and to do that, they need clues about whether they can trust the narrator or whether they might need to doubt the story as it's being told.

Have you created a unique character voice?

When we're writing in first person, we have to subjugate our authorial voice. We are not the one telling this story, and so, for the most part, our voice has no part in it. The voice our reader should hear is the voice of the character telling the story. We're still in control. We created this character, after all, and we can make her sound as much or as little like us as is suitable for the story, but our first-person narrator's voice needs to be paramount.

I'm going to give you a couple of examples so you can hear what I mean.

Example 1:

There was no possibility of taking a walk that day. We had been wandering indeed, in the leafless shrubbery an hour in the morning, but since dinner the cold winter wind had brought with it clouds so somber, and a rain so penetrating, that further outdoor exercise was now out of the question.

I was glad of it: I never liked long walks, especially on chilly afternoons: dreadful to me was the coming home in the raw twilight, with nipped fingers and toes, and a heart saddened by the chidings of Bessie the nurse, and humbled by the consciousness of my physical inferiority to Eliza, John, and Georgiana Reed.

(From *Jane Eyre* by Charlotte Bronte)

From this single passage you can tell this is a character with low self-esteem who sees the world as a hard, unforgiving, often hopeless place. She sees the leafless shrubs, the somber clouds, and the raw twilight.

I'll give you another example so you can hear the difference between them.

Example 2:

There are no cars in the school parking lot when I get there. The place is deserted, which has never bothered me before, but as I cut around the back of the gym, I spot the tree line at the far end of the track and think of the woods and the man with the shovel and the hair at the back of my neck prickles. The weird thing is that the hair isn't rising out of fear. My body is so juiced with adrenaline that when I think of the man, the feeling at the back of my neck is more like the hackles of a vicious dog. I almost want to see him, to dig my fingernails into his face and beat him with my cast. The way I feel at this moment, I think I could kill him.

(From *Cornerstone* by Misty Provencher)

This is a very different character. You can feel the energy in her sentences and the way she rolls one idea into the next. She doesn't pay attention to the weather. And she won't be someone who will back down because she's "chided" by anyone.

One of the best examples of creating unique character voices in first person is Kathryn Stockett's *The Help*, where three distinct first-person narrators tell the story.

Many authors think they've created a unique character voice if they give their character a catch phrase or a dialect quirk, but that's not what *unique character voice* means.

When we talk about character voice, those things do come into play, but what we really mean is that character's unique outlook and personality expressed in their thoughts and speech. Readers enjoy first-person POV in part because of the intimate look at the way another person views the world. Fiction allows us to explore this new perspective in a way we never can in our daily lives.

Before you set out to write a first-person POV story (or when you're trying to revise your first draft), ask yourself these questions:

- How do they view the world around them? (E.g., mostly evil, mostly good, fair, unfair, random, ordered by a bigger plan...)
- How do they view themselves?
- How do they feel about the big-ticket items like love and faith?
- How do they feel about the people closest to them?
- Are they cynical or optimistic?

More might come to you as you answer these. For example, you'll need to know how the perspective of a character who has experienced war will differ from a character who has never known anything but peace. If your character watched their parents endure a nasty divorce, how will their perspective on life and the world and the relationships between men and women be different than will the perspective of a character whose parents were madly in love?

Once you've answered all the questions you can think of, consider how this will affect the tone of what your character says and thinks, the things she comments on, and the little asides she makes to herself. That's where a unique character voice grows.

First person is all about interpretation by the narrator. Or, in some cases, misinterpretation. It's not objective. It can't be any more than we can be entirely objective about our lives and the world around us.

How and what the narrator interprets are important elements of characterization. Showing change in how and what they interpret is an important element of their character arc and growth throughout the book.

Have you shown us not only what they're doing, but also why they're doing it and how they feel about it?

There are two parts to this.

The first part is to make sure you're actually showing us what the narrator is doing and feeling rather than telling us what she did and felt or what she planned to do.

I'll give you an example so you can see it.

> **I** stalked out of the restaurant **to** hail a cab. **I was** furious at him **for** cheating on me again—and in public, where my mother could see him and call me. **I was** going **to** make sure he knew forgiveness wasn't coming this time. By the time he crawled home, **I'd have** changed the locks and packed his belongings and set the boxes in the hall outside our door.

I've bolded some of the warning signs. One of the warning signs of this is a series of I, I, I sentences coupled with state-of-being verbs like *have* and *was*. The words *to* and *for* can also be red flags.

The problem is that we're telling what she plans to do, but we're not actually showing her do anything in that paragraph.

The second part of this question is motivations and reactions. Motivations and reactions are what give first-person POV the intimate feel that's one of its strengths.

Have your first-person narrator respond in their head to something said aloud or jump ahead and make assumptions about what they think the other person will say next. Let us know why they've decided to respond in a certain way. Afterward, show us how what they did is affecting them emotionally and mentally. These chains are more important in first-person POV than in any other.

Have you added variety to your sentences rather than falling into a repetitive pattern of starting almost every sentence with *I*?

This point dovetails with what we just talked about. Beginning almost every sentence with *I* is a common problem when we try to write in first-person POV. This happens more often in first person than in other points of view because of the narcissistic nature of first person. The focus is so tightly on the point of view character and their perception that we can easily fall into a pattern of *I did this and then I did that.*

The problem with this pattern is the same as with any other repetition in fiction. It can quickly bore or annoy the reader. We need to make sure our sentence structure has enough variety to be interesting.

Have you written in scenes?

The temptation when writing first-person POV is for it to almost become stream of consciousness, but we still need to write in scenes. We don't need to see every detail of the POV character's life.

We still only need to see the things important to the story. Each scene should have a goal, we should enter as late as possible, and we should leave as early as possible.

Have you alternated internal with external so the story doesn't feel claustrophobic?

More than any other POV, first-person POV can feel claustrophobic because you're usually trapped in one character's head the whole time. (This is the negative flip side of the intimacy it gives.) And because that character is telling the story directly—in other words, there's no distance at all—it's easy to fall prey to the *talking head syndrome*.

Talking head syndrome is where our character narrates for paragraphs (or even pages) without any external stimuli. The reader starts to feel like the character is just a disembodied head floating in empty space because they don't see, hear, feel, smell, taste, or touch anything happening around them.

Don't put your first-person POV character in a bubble. It's important that we regularly alternate between internal (our character thinking/narrating/feeling) and external (the five senses/action/setting/dialogue).

When we alternate regularly between internal and external, we keep the reader grounded both in the world around them and in the emotions and thoughts of our character.

Does your first-person narrator come across as stupid?

Throughout our book, our first-person POV character will likely miss something important, misinterpret information, or otherwise overlook a clue we've planted.

If we don't want our first-person narrator to come across as stupid when they miss something, we need to create events that could easily have two possible interpretations or a situation where it would be believable for them to have missed that clue.

Having a character who's too stupid to live in third-person POV is annoying. In first-person POV, it can kill the book.

CHAPTER SIX

Third-Person Point of View

THE FINAL POINT OF VIEW TYPE IS third-person POV. In third person, a scene, chapter, or sometimes even the whole book is told from the perspective of a single character, but it uses *he/she* instead of *I*.

> Melanie dug through her purse. No keys. They were here yesterday. She'd dropped them in when she came home from work. Hadn't she? She tipped her purse's contents out onto the table, and receipts, old gum wrappers, and pennies spilled everywhere.

Technically, omniscient POV can also be a third-person point of view because it can use *he/she* as well. For the sake of clarity, from this point on, when I say "third person" I'm meaning limited third person where we're inside the head of one character at a time and where the narrator is a character in the story.

So, in third person, everything is filtered through the eyes of the viewpoint character, and we hear their voice. We can have multiple third-person viewpoint characters per book as long as we don't hop between them in a single scene. (I'll explain head-hopping later on.)

Even though you can have multiple POV characters, try to write your book with the smallest possible number. Few of us are writing something like George R.R. Martin's *Game of Thrones* because it's very difficult to create that many character voices.

Third-person POV can be close (often called deep POV or intimate POV) or it can be more distant. This is your choice based on your vision for your book. (I'll cover narrative distance more in a later chapter as well.)

While it's an option to write in present tense in third person, it's very uncommon because readers tend to find it sounds awkward.

WHAT ARE THE ADVANTAGES OF USING A THIRD-PERSON POINT OF VIEW?

Compared to omniscient and first person POVs, third-person point of view has two main advantages.

First, you can have the intimacy of a first-person POV, but with more flexibility in terms of viewpoint characters. It's also easier to make the viewpoint character clear in third person without having to resort to adding their name to the start of each chapter.

You also have more flexibility in how distinctive each character's voice needs to be. Don't get me wrong. Each viewpoint character still needs to sound distinct from the others, but it's not as drastic as when you're writing in a first-person POV because, in first-person POV, the narrator is speaking directly to the reader.

Second, in a sense, in third-person POV, we, as readers, become each character for the duration of their scenes. We don't do that in a first-person narrative. In a first-person narrative, we're being told the story by the narrator. And that ability to become the characters in third person is one of the greatest strengths of a third-person book and why it's still the most popular POV.

It also means you don't need to think about why the narrator is telling the story. Technically speaking, in a third-person POV book, there isn't a narrator per se. It's more like we're eavesdropping or spying on the characters. We can slip inside them and listen to their thoughts and feel their feelings. They're not aware of our existence.

WHAT ARE THE DISADVANTAGES OF USING THIRD-PERSON POV?

Unfortunately, third person is the easiest of all the POVs to make the mistake of telling about or showing something that the current viewpoint character wouldn't know. In first person, that's a harder mistake to make, because how do you explain the fact that the person talking to the reader is telling them something they couldn't possibly tell them? In omniscient, it's a mistake you can't make because the omniscient narrator knows everything.

Another disadvantage is the temptation to allow too many characters to become the viewpoint character. For example, if you're writing a romance, only the hero, heroine, and maybe the antagonist should be allowed to have scenes from their viewpoint. We don't need scenes from the viewpoint of the heroine's best friend, the hero's mother, and the quirky store clerk who's also secretly in love with the hero. The more viewpoint characters we have in a book, the more difficult it becomes for the reader to connect emotionally to each one of them. This is much less of a temptation in first-person POV and a non-issue entirely with omniscient POV. (We'll take a look at how to choose your viewpoint character and the number of viewpoint characters in Chapters Eleven and Twelve.)

In third-person POV, there's also the danger of switching POVs too often, even in books where we don't have many viewpoint characters numerically speaking. Each viewpoint character should have at least a scene—and it's better if we give them a chapter or two—before we switch to another viewpoint character. If we switch too quickly, it can start to feel choppy to the reader and they don't get a chance to settle in and connect with the character. This whiplash effect is less of a danger in first person, but much more of a danger in omniscient.

HOW ARE FIRST PERSON AND THIRD PERSON SIMILAR?

First-person POV and third-person POV have more in common with each other than either of them do with omniscient in terms of intimacy. If you're writing in a deep or intimate third person, you could change the *he* or *she* to *I* and need very few other changes to make the point-of-view change work.

They also both need to maintain consistency to the viewpoint character. If you fail to maintain consistency, you have a POV error.

With that in mind, it's time to look at head-hopping and other point-of-view errors.

CHAPTER SEVEN

Head-Hopping vs. Omniscient POV

WE NEED TO BE CLEAR ABOUT something right up front: head-hopping is never good. Sometimes an author can get away with it, but it's never ideal and it never makes your story stronger. Never. Just because you sometimes catch a bestselling author do it doesn't mean their book wouldn't be stronger without it as well.

Omniscient POV, on the other hand, is a valid point of view for fiction. It might not be the most popular or the most commonly used in twenty-first century fiction, but there's nothing wrong with it. And some stories are even best told in it. A story written in omniscient POV can be absolutely fantastic when done well.

So I'm going to explain how head-hopping and omniscient POV differ, then I'll give you a rubric you can apply when you're not sure what you have on your hands.

Difference #1 - Omniscient POV Uses One Viewpoint, Head-Hopping Uses Many

In an omniscient POV story, the only viewpoint is that of the narrator. You don't switch viewpoints between characters. The only "eyes" you'll ever see the story through are the eyes of the omniscient narrator. That narrator is all-knowing, so they can peel back the skull of any character and show you what's happening inside, but you'll never experience the story through the perspective of any of those characters. Their opinions won't color the narrative.

In head-hopping, the author slides between different viewpoint characters without a proper transition. *Without a proper transition* is important. You can have multiple viewpoint characters within a single story, and you can switch between them. You just can't switch between them without a proper transition. I'll explain proper transitions later in this chapter.

If you think of point of view as a camera, then the location of the camera is different. In omniscient POV, the camera is always outside of the characters, looking down on them. In head-hopping, the camera is inside of multiple characters at once, almost like you have a split screen.

Difference #2 – Omniscient POV Uses One Voice, Head-Hopping Uses Many

In omniscient POV, the only voice you will ever hear outside of dialogue and direct internal dialogue (internal dialogue that's written in first person, present tense and italicized) is the narrator. It doesn't matter what character the scene focuses on—you'll still hear only that single voice. The sentence structure, word choices, etc. won't change. The *Harry Potter* books are an excellent example of this. The voice is consistent throughout the entire series because it's the narrator's voice, not the characters' voices, telling the story.

In head-hopping, you'll have many different voices to suit the different characters. (You'll also have many different voices in properly written third-person POV where you have multiple viewpoint characters. This is why understanding the *without a proper transition* element of head-hopping is so important.)

A FRAMEWORK FOR DISTINGUISHING BETWEEN THE TWO

I want to distill this down for you into a clear guideline you can use for figuring out whether you're looking at omniscient POV or head-hopping.

To be head-hopping, a passage needs to meet two criteria:

1) The viewpoint shifts between characters without a proper transition.

2) The thoughts/feelings of the characters are given in their voices rather than in the author's voice or the omniscient narrator's voice.

It's really that simple. If you give the flavor of a particular character's voice, and switch viewpoints without a proper transition, you're head-hopping.

Now that you know the definition of head-hopping, you'll be able to run everything through its filter to decide if a passage is head-hopping or genuinely omniscient POV.

Omniscient POV will be written in the omniscient narrator's voice. The characters' feelings and thoughts will be filtered through the narrator.

Head-hopping will be in the characters' voices, and you'll go back and forth without a proper transition.

Let me give you an example of head hopping so you can see it in action...

Jack rolled down the window half an inch, a smirk spreading across his face. The slut would never find her way back without him, and no one would find her until the coyotes had picked her bones clean.

Anna yanked at the door handle. Her chest felt heavy, her lungs unwilling to suck in a full breath. "Unlock the door, Jake. This isn't funny anymore."

Jake's cold blue eyes stared into hers. After all she'd made him suffer through, he was going to enjoy this moment. Savor it like a medium rare T-bone steak.

Now let's break it apart.

Jack rolled down the window half an inch, a smirk spreading across his face.

Sounds like we're in someone else's viewpoint here. Someone who's watching Jake. If we were in Jake's viewpoint, this would read *Jake rolled down the window half an inch and smirked.* It might seem like a small difference, but if we're in Jake's viewpoint, he's acting. If we're in someone else's viewpoint, we're watching Jake's body language from the outside. The perspective on what's happening is different depending on where we're standing.

The slut would never find her way back without him, and no one would find her until the coyotes had picked her bones clean.

We're hearing Jake's thoughts in Jake's voice. It's him, not the author, thinking of Anna as a slut.

Anna yanked at the door handle. Her chest felt heavy, her lungs unwilling to suck in a full breath.

Now we're firmly in Anna's head. Only she can describe how her chest feels and the dread settling there.

"Unlock the door, Jake. This isn't funny anymore."
Jake's cold blue eyes stared into hers.

We're still in Anna's viewpoint since she's the one who can see Jake's eye color.

After all she'd made him suffer through, he was going to enjoy this moment. Savor it like a rare T-bone steak.

Jake's thoughts in Jake's voice again.

WHY IS HEAD-HOPPING A PROBLEM?

Head hopping damages your story because it makes the writing feel choppy. Readers constantly need to pause, however slightly, and figure out who they're supposed to identify with. They're often left feeling disconnected entirely. Even if they don't know what to call head-hopping, they'll know something is off and that they have a difficult time connecting emotionally with the characters/narrator(s). Readers need to connect emotionally with either the characters (in first-person POV and third-person POV) or with the author/narrator (in omniscient POV).

WHAT COUNTS AS A PROPER TRANSITION?

At the beginning of this chapter, I told you that one of the criteria for head-hopping was that the viewpoint shifts between characters without a proper transition. This begs the question of what qualifies as a proper transition compared to an improper transition.

Improper Transitions

I've shown how switching viewpoints within a paragraph is head-hopping, but switching viewpoints between paragraphs is also an improper transition. If we're writing in first person or third person, we can't use one viewpoint character in our first paragraph and then switch to another viewpoint character in the next paragraph. That's still head-hopping.

As a way around this, some authors use what's called a baton pass.

A baton pass happens when we use an object in the environment to signal a viewpoint shift between two characters. I've bolded the baton pass in the following passage.

> Emily dropped two sugar cubes into the bottom of the mug and poured in the steaming tea. Heaven forbid her mother be asked to add the sugar cubes after the tea was in the cup like a normal person would. Thank God she only had to deal with her mother's quirks on holidays anymore. **She pushed the cup across the table to her mother.**
>
> **Alice accepted the cup and swirled the tea around inside.** If the look on Emily's face at having to prepare the tea the proper way was any indication, her next request was going to go over about as well as if she asked the ungrateful girl to slit her own wrists. "I've been to see the doctor again, and the news isn't good."

In this passage, we switch viewpoint characters from Emily to her mother Alice, using the mug of tea as our baton.

I have this listed as an improper transition because most people, myself included, consider a baton pass to be an insufficient transition to justify a change in the viewpoint character.

You will occasionally see a big-name author do it. But just because they can sometimes get away with it doesn't mean we should try it. It doesn't even mean they should. No matter how well it's done, a baton pass is confusing to the reader and causes them to hesitate.

Proper Transitions

For proper transitions, I'm going to move from the most clear and obvious to a more subtle method.

So the first way to properly transition between viewpoint characters is simply to switch during a chapter break. This is the easiest for the reader to handle because they have to slightly reorient themselves between chapters anyway. It doesn't seem jarring to be in a new point of view when a new chapter starts.

A very similar situation is when we have a scene break within a chapter. Scene breaks are often marked with asterisks or some other symbol. When we do this, we need to be careful that our scenes are long enough and that we don't switch viewpoint characters every scene. We want our reader to have a chance to settle in.

Sometimes, though, we need to switch our viewpoint within a scene. We can do this as long as we insert a blank line. That's an indicator to the reader to expect a switch. Do this very sparingly, as it can feel like the scene has stopped dead in order for us to swap viewpoint characters. (Some authors will use asterisks or some other symbol to signify these switches as well, since they're easier to spot than a blank line. That's fine too, and it's actually my personal preference. When in doubt, I like to err on the side of clarity.)

The final way to transition is to use a camera zoom out. This is tricky for new writers to master, so my advice is that if you want to do this, pay attention to how it's handled in published works.

What basically happens here is that, for a minute, we're going to be disembodied. The reader is going to leave the current viewpoint character's head, float without attachment for a sentence or two, and then reconnect to another viewpoint character. We usually only want to do this when we're changing the location as well.

Let me show you how it looks.

> Elaine twirled the dial on the safe and the door popped. Finally. Three months of work, but it was all going to be worth it once she got her hands on those files. She swung the door open. The safe was empty.
>
> **Across town, her former partner leaned over the phone records and photos that proved the senator's infidelities.** Grant waited for his digital camera to focus and snapped close-up images of the first paper. He couldn't keep a smile from his lips. What he wouldn't give to see Elaine's face when she found the safe empty. Served her right for cutting him out of this job.

That single bolded sentence is a camera zoom out. For that single sentence, we're on the move and not connected to a character just for the duration of the transition. As soon as we hit Grant, we're right back in his head and his viewpoint.

Camera zoom outs need to be used strategically. We need to ask ourselves whether we really need them or if we could simply drop in a scene or chapter break and end up with the same result.

CHAPTER EIGHT

How to Maintain a Consistent Viewpoint

HEAD-HOPPING IS ONE POSSIBLE ERROR when it comes to point of view, but we can also make errors that have nothing to do with head-hopping. These point-of-view errors are actually more common than head-hopping, especially once a writer passes from new to intermediate.

POV errors happen any time we're in a limited point of view—where we're supposed to stay inside one viewpoint character at a time—and we write something that our viewpoint character couldn't know or wouldn't be thinking about.

To avoid these point of view errors, follow one guideline: **You are the viewpoint character**.

I know that might sound simplistic, but if you actually embrace this and execute it, you won't have any point-of-view errors in your book.

However, understanding a concept and being able to properly execute it are two different things. Because of how important this concept is, we're going to focus on it in the next two chapters.

To start, I'm going to break down into steps what becoming your viewpoint character means.

YOU KNOW WHAT THEY KNOW

If they don't know it, we can't write about it.

This is foundational. We can only write what our viewpoint character knows.

No "little did she know" or any similar statements blatantly forecasting or foretelling the future. Our viewpoint character can't know what's coming in the future unless he's a prophet having a vision.

No telling what other characters are thinking or feeling (unless, of course, our character is a telepath or has ESP).

We also can't tell the reader *why* another character did something. The internal motivation of other characters is unknown to our viewpoint character.

So, for example, we can't write a sentence like...

Her movement caught Eddie's eye, and he turned to face her.

If the *she* mentioned in this sentence is the viewpoint character, she can't know why Eddie turned to face her. She doesn't know if it was her movement, a sound she made, or if he was going to turn in that direction anyway.

Here's another one. We're going to continue with the female character as the viewpoint character. Eddie is not our viewpoint character in this example.

Eddie's mouth fell open **at the sight of her**.

Again, she can't know why Eddie's mouth fell open. Therefore, the "at the sight of her" is a POV error.

We could rewrite this as...

Eddie turned to face her and his mouth fell open.

We haven't lost anything from the meaning, but we've removed the POV error by sticking to including only what our viewpoint character can know.

This guideline also applies to the word choices our character makes. For example, if we have a male character who knows nothing about fashion, he won't be able to describe our female character's shoes as Jimmy Choos or her dress as a Vera Wang knock-off.

If we have a character who has never seen a shovel before, not even in pictures, she won't be able to call it a shovel. She'll have no frame of reference to do so. She'll come up with her own ideas of what to call it and her own ideas of what it's for (at least until she learns its proper name).

YOU SENSE WHAT THEY SENSE

If they can't see it, hear it, touch it, taste it, or smell it, neither can we.

For example, if Andrea is our viewpoint character, writing "Andrea's face turned red" is a POV mistake. You can't see your own face. What we could write instead is "Andrea's face burned" or "Heat rushed up Andrea's neck."

This also means we experience events at the same time that our viewpoint character experiences them.

For example, when you describe another character's voice before they speak, that's a POV error because your character hasn't heard the tone they're going to speak in yet.

I'll give you an example. We're still in Andrea's viewpoint for this one.

His voice turned gravelly. "How did you know that?"

If we're in Andrea's head, there's no way she can know his voice turned gravelly before he speaks in the gravelly voice.

YOU THINK WHAT THEY THINK

Our viewpoint character won't think about something that they've regularly seen or experienced because their mind already skims over it. They have no need to explain or mull over items they interact with on a regular basis because they know how those items work and what they look like. They can use them without thinking about it.

For example, do you regularly think about the color of your eyes? You probably don't think about your hair or eye color much at all, or the type of house you live in (unless you come home to find that your husband and his friends have knocked out a wall), or about the way your boss regularly dresses. You don't think about how to use a telephone or turn on your computer. You don't think about the set-up of your society either—you take that for granted.

I commonly see this problem come up when a writer either describes what their viewpoint character is wearing long after they've put those clothes on or describes their attire at another time when they wouldn't be thinking about their clothes.

I'll give you a quick example. In the book I'm working on with Lisa Hall-Wilson, we wrote this about our main character:

She pushed against the familiar binding constricting her breasts, her hair in a warrior's tail down her back.

We'd made a POV mistake. Why would she be thinking about her hair in a warrior's tail down her back? We'd meant it as her doing a checklist, but it wasn't coming across that way to readers.

Here's the change we made:

> She pushed against the binding constricting her breasts, and tightened the tie fastening her hair in a warrior's tail down her back.

A small change, but it erased the POV violation.

I also commonly see this happening when a writer writes something like...

> Her younger sister Marianne grabbed the book from her hands.

If she's our viewpoint character, she already knows Marianne is her younger sister and she has no reason to think about it.

This can often happen in a slightly different form when we're trying to avoid overuse of a character's name. Say, for example, we have a character named Father Andrew Matthany. We might end up calling him *the priest, Andrew, Father Andrew, Father Matthany,* or *the man.*

The reason this ends up being a point-of-view error is that most people have a single way they think of and refer to another person in their thoughts. (Besides being a POV error, we should be consistent in what we call our characters because it can be confusing for readers otherwise.)

This becomes a POV error from the other side as well. If our viewpoint character is young teacher Janice Harwood, then it would be an error to write something like this...

> The window at the front of her classroom shattered. Janice ducked under her desk. The young teacher curled into a

ball and covered her head with her arms. Thank goodness
all the children had made it out before the storm hit.

Janice isn't going to think about herself as "the young teacher."

This idea extends further out, again, to the language our view-point character would use to describe something they do think about. How they feel about that thing will come through in the wording they choose. For example, in the *Harry Potter* series, the villain went from being called *He-Who-Must-Not-Be-Named* when there was fear of him to *Voldemort* when they began to stand up and fight him. The progression to this point was natural. The use of the two names wasn't a random swapping back and forth in order to avoid overusing a single name.

As another example, would you think about your hair as your "raven tresses"? Probably not, even if you did think about your black hair.

Including only what our viewpoint character would think about also helps us solve the problem of when and how much backstory to insert. We put in backstory when our character would naturally be thinking about it (due to an external trigger) and they only think about it briefly. For example, we don't tend to stop in the middle of something else and stand around for ten minutes reliving the entire break-up with our ex. A thought passes through our mind about only the single aspect that's pertinent to our present situation.

I'm not going to go into internal dialogue too much because this book is on point of view and internal dialogue is a book in itself, but when it comes to your viewpoint character's internal dialogue (in other words, what they're thinking), it needs to pass the three-question test.

Question #1 - Would my character think this?

I mentioned this briefly above, but do you normally mull over things like the color of your carpet? I don't. I also don't think about the color of my best friend's hair (because I've seen it so many times). I don't think about the sound my truck makes or even what route to take to get home.

If our character doesn't care about it, they won't think about it. If our character wouldn't think about it, it's a point-of-view error. We can't try to sneak in information through internal dialogue, no matter how important we think it is.

Question #2 - Is this the way they'd think it?

If our internal dialogue passes the first test, we still need to ask if they'd think about it in the way we've written it.

Let's say I would be thinking about my truck because it starts to make a strange noise while I'm driving home. I'm likely to worry about whether I'm going to get stranded on the side of the road in the dark. Or about where we'll get the money for repairs if something is wrong.

If my dad is driving my truck and hears a strange noise, he's going to describe it in words I'd never think of (a rattle, a grind, a whine, a screech), and he's going to think about what the causes could be. He knows the parts of an engine or the braking system.

But it goes further than this. What tone would they use in this situation?

Question #3 - Would they be thinking this <u>now</u>?

Context is everything. On a normal day, I might hear that noise and think about it. If there's a man with a gun in the seat next to me, I'm not going to think about that noise unless there's a way I think I can leverage it to get away.

If you'd like to learn more about internal dialogue, check out my book *Internal Dialogue: A Busy Writer's Guide.*

YOU INTERPRET THE WORLD THE WAY THEY INTERPRET THE WORLD

This one's a little trickier, but it comes down to judgment and perception. Our viewpoint character isn't an objective observer of the world around them. They're subjective. Everything they see and experience ends up filtered through their opinions and their personality.

I'll break this down into some questions to help us see what this means in practical application.

Is this the way a person of their time period, gender, and social status would perceive the world?

Like it or not, these three elements are intertwined. The way a woman from upper-class 1700s Britain viewed the world will not be the same as the way a 1960s flower child viewed the world.

Even apart from how gender questions interact with time periods, anachronisms can easily sneak in if we're not careful. For example, we're now aware of the health risks involved with smoking cigarettes. If our character lives in the first half of the 1900s, however, they won't see smoking as a health risk. They might not like the smell or the way it yellows teeth, but they're not going to be thinking about second-hand smoke or lung cancer. They might even smoke themselves if everyone else from their social circle does. They might not understand their craving for it as an addiction.

Our characters can be outliers in their society as well, but what we need to keep in mind is that most people aren't outliers in everything. A wealthy Southern woman pre-Civil War might be against slavery and yet still conform to all the other ethics and conventions of her time period and station. Most people aren't in opposition to everything around them. Most of us are instead molded by our upbringing and society, and selectively choose which parts to rebel against based—again—on our personal experiences.

If we want our character to be an outlier in some respect, we need to know *why* they are this way. What event(s) formed this renegade belief system? It's not enough to have them interpret the world this way because we want them to. It needs to come from inside them.

Is this the word or phrase our character would choose to use?

I won't linger over this point because we've already look at it before, but I will give you an example.

My grandparents refer to African-Americans as colored people. Most of us nowadays cringe away from that phrasing because of the connotations, but for people of my grandparents' generation, that was simply common parlance. They had many black friends and weren't in the least bit racist. The terminology doesn't carry the same meaning for them.

We need to be careful to choose the word our character would use, even if that isn't a term or phrase we'd personally want to use. If we were writing a story with characters like my grandparents in it, we'd be violating their viewpoint to have them use a different term.

Is this the way our character would judge and react to the other people in the scene?

The snap judgments our viewpoint character comes to during their first impression of a person aren't something they can control. Those are conditioned responses. What our viewpoint character thinks about others tells us less about those people and more about our viewpoint character. What we personally would think about those people, in the same situation, doesn't matter.

For example, what is our viewpoint character's automatic reaction to a biker? Are they frightened? Fascinated? What would they do if a prostitute sat at their table in a restaurant? Would they try to hire them? Give a faith witness to them? Buy them dinner just to be nice, with no ulterior motives?

How does our character feel about the man driving a Rolls-Royce? Do they envy him? Or find it wasteful when there are starving children in the world? Do they attribute his car to being a reward for success or to vanity and a need to compensate for low self-esteem?

This goes even beyond this, digging into how your character positions themselves in the world. By necessity, our world separates into *us* and *them*. Think back to your high school experience if you want to see this in action. If you were a band geek, you likely weren't also a member of the football team. You were on the inside of one group (the *us*) and on the outside of another (the *them*).

These positional relationships are sometimes ones we can't even control. If you're a man, you're not also a woman. If you're rich, you're not also poor. If you're 100% Caucasian, you're not also Asian or Native American.

An important part of our character's viewpoint is how they position themselves in relation to others.

Additional Tip: If you're a science fiction or fantasy author, thinking about the different groups of people and how they interact can be a goldmine for world-building.

What would our character notice about the setting? How would they describe it?

Your character will only notice and describe things that matter to them. If something that wouldn't normally matter to them is important to the story, you need to find a believable reason for them to notice it.

How our viewpoint character feels about the setting should also come through in how they describe it. They'll describe someplace they love using different words than they will for a place they despise. Everything, *everything*, we include says something about our viewpoint character. And this is one of the main reasons we want to avoid generic descriptions (along with the fact that generic descriptions are boring).

What would be new or old to our character?

How our viewpoint character interprets the world around them shows the reader what's normal in the world and what isn't. So if you want elephants riding bicycles to be normal, then your viewpoint character won't act surprised, might barely notice it, when they have to step out of the way of a bicycle-riding elephant. They might even be grumpy about it and wish that the legislation requiring bike-riding licenses had gone through, but the fact that elephants are the ones on the bikes won't be remarked upon (unless elephants are notoriously terrible bike riders).

On the opposite end, if something new to our viewpoint character enters the scene, we can't skim over it. We're drawn to things that are new. Our brains need to categorize them and understand them.

The foundation of all of this is that our characters should interpret the world for themselves. Our interpretation of the world around them and the events in it doesn't matter. We can't foist our beliefs onto characters if those beliefs don't fit them.

YOU, AS THE AUTHOR, DON'T GET TO INTRUDE INTO THE WORLD

We're going to look at author intrusion more in a later chapter, but here it is in a nutshell.

In a limited point of view, the author doesn't get to intrude into the world. Ever. Period. We should be 100% invisible.

In first-person or third-person POV, any time we as the author show up, for any reason, it's a POV error.

Let's say, for example, that we have Allan and Becky. Allan has just told Becky that he's not going to apply for a better position that came open at work.

> Becky frowned and set aside her fork. "Why not?"
> Allan shrugged. "I don't know."
> When Allan was a little boy, his father was always running him down and telling him how stupid he was. Even though his old man had been dead for ten years, Allan's self-esteem had never bounced back.

All that stuff after Allan's dialogue is author intrusion.

If we follow these guidelines and run any potential POV errors through that analysis, we'll be able to avoid POV errors. Since POV errors can be tricky to spot, though, I'll show you some sneaky POV errors in the next chapter. We'll also take this concept further in Chapter Ten by talking about narrative distance and author intrusion.

CHAPTER NINE

Sneaky Point-of-View Errors and How to Fix Them

P OINT-OF-VIEW ERRORS CAN BE SOME OF the trickiest to spot, even if you know the guidelines I laid out in the previous chapter. The purpose of this chapter is to show you a whole list of sneaky point-of-view errors and explain why they're errors.

Once we see examples and understand why those examples count as point-of-view errors, suddenly they become much easier to catch in our own work. We're likely to still write them during our drafting phase, but we'll be able to correct them during self-editing.

I'll separate these errors out into some general categories to help you understand the bigger underlying issues that create these point-of-view errors. You can think about this as coming at the material in the last chapter from a different direction. Sometimes it can help us understand a concept better if we look at it from multiple angles.

At the end of this chapter, I'll also give you some guiding principles for fixing point-of-view errors and the little-known secret for understanding and catching point-of-view errors.

ATTRIBUTING EMOTIONS TO NON-VIEWPOINT CHARACTERS

In the last chapter, I pointed out that we can only include what our viewpoint character knows. One area where it's easy to violate point of view is in the emotions of other, non-viewpoint characters.

Katie watched him sadly.

If our viewpoint character is someone other than Katie, then our viewpoint character can't know that Katie is watching sadly. The fix for something like this is to simply describe the evidence.

e.g., Katie watched him, blinking rapidly, her lips turned down.

Dan kept his attention on the bomb, unfazed by the ticking clock.

If Dan isn't our viewpoint character, our viewpoint character can't know whether Dan is fazed or unfazed. Dan might seem unfazed on the outside, but he might be barely keeping his calm on the inside.

ATTRIBUTING MOTIVATION TO A NON-VIEWPOINT CHARACTER

I'm going to include the most examples in this section because this is the sneaky point-of-view error I see the most often.

POINT OF VIEW | 79

When I talk about attributing motivations, what I mean is telling the reader *why* a character did something. Within our viewpoint character, sharing motivations is an important element of fiction that's clear and resonates emotionally with the reader. But when we instead start to share the motivation of a non-viewpoint character (in other words, share the reason a non-viewpoint character did something), then we're creating a point-of-view error.

Everything is easier to understand once we've seen some examples, so here we go.

> Her movement caught Eddie's eye, and he turned to face her.

You should remember this one from the previous chapter. If the *she* mentioned in this sentence is the viewpoint character, she can't know why Eddie turned to face her. She doesn't know if it was her movement, a sound she made, or if he was going to turn in that direction anyway.

> Eddie's mouth fell open at the sight of her.

You should remember this one from the previous chapter as well. If she's the viewpoint character, she can't know why Eddie's mouth fell open. Therefore, the "at the sight of her" is a POV error.

> Franklin tapped his foot. With slow, deliberate strokes, Johnny sharpened his ax, preparing to drop a tree onto the road into the convoy's path.

Like all the previous examples, what makes a POV error here is whose mind we're supposed to be in. If we're in Franklin's viewpoint, then "preparing to drop a tree onto the road" is a POV error. Franklin can't know for sure that Johnny is preparing to drop a tree onto the road using his ax. Johnny might be preparing to chop up

Franklin because he's finally snapped after being treated like a slave rather than a partner. Johnny might be preparing to use the ax as a weapon when he attacks the convoy. The point is that Franklin can't know what's happening inside Johnny's head and what Johnny's motivation is for sharpening the ax.

> James scowled at Christine and reached over to brush dirt off her shirt sleeve.

If Christine is our viewpoint character, then she can't know why James reached over until he actually does it. We're telling why he did something, but we're not showing him do it. We show the reaching here, but not the brushing. Errors like this one are extremely easy to fix.

E.g., James scowled at Christine, reached over, and brushed dirt off her shirt sleeve.

TELLING THE READER WHAT A NON-VIEWPOINT CHARACTER THOUGHT OR SAW

Head-hopping isn't the only point-of-view error that invades a non-viewpoint character's body. It happens more subtly when we do something like what's shown in the following examples.

> He thought about that for a minute.

If the thinker isn't the viewpoint character, this is a point-of-view error. The POV character can't know the person is thinking about what they've said or that they're thinking at all. One way to fix this would be to give the character an action that might imply thinking, such as frowning or rubbing their upper lip.

Other variations of this include saying a non-viewpoint character is considering, realizing, believing, etc.

Evelyn noticed the boy dressed as a clown and laughed.

If our viewpoint character is someone other than Evelyn, our
viewpoint character can't know that Evelyn notices the boy and that
that causes her to laugh.

To fix this, we'd need to give our viewpoint character something
they can see. So, for example, we could have Evelyn laugh (without
explaining the cause), then have her point to the boy.

INCLUDING ITEMS THE VIEWPOINT CHARACTER DOESN'T NOTICE OR CAN'T SEE

The biggest POV offenders in this category tend to be those actions that happen without conscious thought—for example, if we're
very upset and we grip our paper cup so tightly we crush it, not realizing until we calm down that we've done so. If we're the viewpoint
character, we could only describe that crushed paper cup once we do
realize what we've done.

Let me show you a few more examples (including one where the
character literally can't see what's being described rather than that
he's simply unaware of it).

Unknowingly, she tightened her grip on his arm.

If *she* is the viewpoint character, this is an error. She doesn't
know she tightened her grip on his arm, so we can't show it. The
way to fix this would be to instead show his reaction to the tighten-
ing and then have her learn she'd tightened her grip.

> Karen turned to look out the window and didn't notice Jeff slip the business card into his pocket.

If Karen is our viewpoint character, then we can't record anything she didn't see or notice. The way around this one would be to show Karen noticing later that the business card is missing or, if we also use Jeff's viewpoint, to show after he leaves that he pocketed the business card.

A similar POV error to this one is when we forget that we've had our character close their eyes, and we describe movement happening that they couldn't see. Like this...

> Mark dropped down onto the curb and covered his face with his hands. Other pedestrians dodged around him and stared.

Our viewpoint character, Mark, has his eyes covered by his hands. He can't see other people skirting around him and he can't see their stares.

TELLING THE READER WHAT THE VIEWPOINT CHARACTER LOOKS LIKE

We covered this concept in depth in the last chapter, so I'll give just one more example here.

> A pained expression crossed Evelyn's face.

Evelyn is our viewpoint character in this example, and so she can't see her own expression. We can fix this by switching over to what Evelyn feels like inside. Or we can say something like...

> Evelyn grimaced.

We know when we grimace, and it's an action, so this isn't a POV error.

VIOLATING THE TEMPORAL ORDER

Cause and effect, or action and reaction, are foundational concepts for excellent fiction. They undergird almost everything, and that holds true for point of view. If we're solidly within our viewpoint character, then we need to show what's happening as if it were playing out in real time in front of the reader. That means that everything needs to go on the page in the order it would actually happen, and the cause needs to come before the effect it creates.

I'll show you some examples of how we violate this.

His voice turned gravelly. "How did you know that?"

This example is from the previous chapter. Our viewpoint character can't know his voice is about to turn gravelly until he speaks in the gravelly voice.

She threw her arms up when the man reached for her.

She's our viewpoint character. The man reaching for her is the motivation for her reaction. It's what causes her to throw up her arms. Because of that, it needs to come first. She can't know she needs to throw up her arms until she sees him reaching for her.

E.g., The man reached for her, and she threw up her arms.

GUIDING PRINCIPLES FOR FIXING POINT-OF-VIEW ERRORS

Hopefully you'll now be better able to see these point-of-view errors when they show up in your writing, but that's only half of what we need. We also need to know how to fix them. Some of those fixes are easy or obvious ones I pointed out when we were looking at our examples. For the rest, there are three main ways to deal with point-of-view errors.

Describe the action and allow the reader to fill in the blanks using the surrounding context.

In other words, take out the problematic phrase and leave only the objective description of the event.

Whenever possible, this is the best option for resolving point-of-view errors. In my book *Showing and Telling in Fiction*, I explained that the difference between showing and telling is that showing gives the evidence and telling dictates a conclusion. We can apply the same principle here. Show the reader the evidence and allow them to draw a conclusion from it rather than dictating a conclusion for them.

Let's take a quick look at how this plays out in an example. We'll have the characters Sherry and Tom. Sherry is our viewpoint character.

> "I know this isn't what you wanted to hear," Sherry said.
> Tom shrugged off her touch and turned away to avoid looking at her.

Sherry can't know that Tom turned away to avoid looking at her, so that becomes a POV error. And we don't even need it in the sentence.

> "I know this isn't what you wanted to hear," Sherry said.
> Tom shrugged off her touch and turned away.

Sometimes, correcting the POV error will also require us to add or change a little more in the way of context. We'll stick with Sherry and Tom, with Sherry as our viewpoint character.

Tom was saddened. "How could you do this to me?

Telling the reader Tom's emotion of sadness is a POV error. We could change this to show the evidence of his sadness instead.

Tom hunched his shoulders, and he slowly shook his head. "How could you do this to me?" His voice cracked on the last word.

The reader will be able to figure out that Tom is sad based on the evidence.

As long as the context surrounding the situation is clear, our readers will be smart enough to figure it out for themselves.

This also allows us the ability to play with false impressions and misinterpretations if we want to.

Allow the viewpoint character to interpret (and make it clear they're interpreting).

Interpretation of other people's actions is something we all understand because it's something we all do. We can't possibly be in the mind of anyone else, so we have to guess what's going on inside of them. The fun part of this for us as fiction writers is that our characters might be mistaken in their interpretation. (That's not quite as fun when it happens to us in real life.)

We'll go back to Sherry and Tom again. Here's the original.

"I know this isn't what you wanted to hear," Sherry said.
Tom shrugged off her touch and turned away to avoid looking at her.

Now here's an option for what we could do using character interpretation.

"I know this isn't what you wanted to hear," Sherry said.

Tom shrugged off her touch and turned away.

An ache started deep in her belly and expanded up into her chest. Could he not even stand to look at her anymore?

Sherry isn't telling us that Tom couldn't stand to look at her. This is what she thinks is happening.

Show the reader how the viewpoint character knows something that would otherwise be considered a POV error.

This is an extension of the last solution. In this solution, the viewpoint character is still going to be interpreting, but it's more like an educated guess, so they're also going to share why they've come to this conclusion.

I'll move away from Sherry and Tom for this example to a new couple. The woman is our first-person narrator. In this example, our viewpoint character is going to state that her husband is afraid. What makes it work is that she also shows the evidence of how she draws this conclusion.

His hands shook so slightly that I wouldn't have noticed it had he not picked up the tea cup. Just a ripple on the surface of the liquid. The clink of the china bumping his top teeth.

My throat closed, and I couldn't choke down what remained in my own cup. He was afraid. I'd never seen my husband afraid before, not in all our ten years of marriage, not in all the times we'd traveled to hostile locations, not even when he caught malaria and almost died that month we spent in Africa.

We need to be careful with this because we're doubling up on showing and telling. Technically, showing and telling the same thing is repetitious, but when it's used strategically, in moments when we want to emphasize an important element, it can work well.

THE SECRET BEHIND POINT-OF-VIEW ERRORS

I'm about to pull back the wizard's curtain for you when it comes to point-of-view errors and share a secret that many writers don't know.

Here it is: Most point-of-view errors are simply the flip side of telling rather than showing.

What is telling when looked at from inside our viewpoint character becomes a POV error when approached from a non-viewpoint character. So if you understand the difference between telling and showing, you'll be better prepared to also spot point-of-view errors.

I'll show you a couple of examples so you can see what I mean. I'll put the telling/POV error in bold.

Elizabeth went to the woodshed **to get the axe**.

When Elizabeth is our viewpoint character, this is telling. We're told why she planned to go to the woodshed, but we don't see her actually get the axe.

When Elizabeth isn't our viewpoint character, this is a point-of-view error. Our viewpoint character can't know for sure why Elizabeth went to the woodshed. Maybe she was going in there to cry. Or maybe she planned to crawl out the back window and run away.

I'll give one more example.

Eric stalked out of the room, **too angry to listen to any more**.

When Eric is our viewpoint character, this is telling. We've told the reader that he's angry. We haven't shown his anger (or, you might argue, that we've shown and told it since we did show him stalking to the window).

When Eric isn't our viewpoint character, this is a point-of-view error. Our viewpoint character can't know that Eric is too angry to continue to listen.

(If you want to learn more about showing and telling in fiction, or if you're confused by what I mean by *telling*, please take a look at my book *Showing and Telling in Fiction: A Busy Writer's Guide*.)

CHAPTER TEN

Narrative Distance, Author Intrusion, and Telling

THE POPULARITY OF DEEP POV HAS CAUSED some confusion among writers over the difference between narrative distance, author intrusion, and telling. To a newer writer, especially one who is most comfortable in deep POV, they can all seem like the same thing. They're not.

It's also a mistake to assume that deep POV is the only way to write. It's not. Deep POV has become the preferred narrative distance for many genres, but it's not our only option.

To fully understand point of view and make the right choice for our story, we need to also understand narrative distance because it influences the tone, the voice, and the emotional "heat" of our writing. So in this chapter, I'm going to explain what narrative distance means and how it differs from both author intrusion and telling.

NARRATIVE DISTANCE

Narrative distance is basically how close we are to the characters. To put this another way, it's a measure of how different the reader's perspective is from the character's perspective.

At a far narrative distance, we're outside of the characters, observing them. Stories written in far narrative distance include fewer character thoughts and almost no internal visceral reactions. When the narrator does share internalizations by the characters, they're given using filtering words.

At a close narrative distance, we're inside the characters, experiencing the world through their eyes and perspective, as if we were them. It includes more internal dialogue (character thoughts) and more internal, visceral reactions, and we want to show more than tell and avoid filtering words when writing with close narrative distance.

The question of narrative distance is also at the heart of understanding the difference between character voice and author voice. The farther our narrative distance, the more authorial voice we use. The closer the narrative distance, the more character voice we use. (The exception to this, of course, is when we've created a narrator character for our omniscient book, like we see in *The Book Thief*.)

As might be obvious by now, narrative distance is a continuum.

On one end is omniscient point of view and on the other end is first-person point of view. In the middle falls third-person point of view, and this is where most authors end up confused.

Third-person POV is where we can slide along the scale depending on our personal taste and the type of story we want to tell. We can write in deep POV, which has the same—almost non-existence— narrative distance as first person POV. Or we can create a cooler, less emotional feel by drawing back and creating a slightly greater narrative distance.

Writing in a more distant third person still doesn't give us permission to head-hop or insert information that our viewpoint character couldn't have known. All distance does is give a different feel to our writing. The closer we go, the more intense and intimate the writing will feel.

NARRATIVE DISTANCE COMPARED TO TELLING

If we choose to write in a far narrative distance, then we have a narrow line to walk. Far narrative distance can cause us to tell rather than show and suck the life from our fiction. The best way I can explain this to you is to show you some examples of varying narrative distance and then show you telling so we can compare and analyze what makes each of these examples what they are.

Far Narrative Distance

I'm going to start about as far out in narrative distance as we can go.

> The morning sun beat down on the empty meadow, baking all the bushes into bare sticks and leaving nowhere for the two runaways to hide. The man glanced behind them and sighed, as if he'd already given up hope of them successfully escaping. The little girl with him drooped against his side, half walking, half carried, exhausted by a night of running rather than sleeping.
>
> His sister had begged him to take the girl when he burrowed out. The gated communities were no place to raise a child. The Bannari had no qualms about putting them to work in the fields or the bedroom almost as soon as they could walk.

So he'd agreed, but now the extra responsibility of safe-guarding her life weighed him down. They couldn't stop, and she couldn't go on much farther.

Trackers will find us 'fore we even fall asleep if we try to make camp out here, he thought. *We have to reach the trees.*

She stumbled and the man steadied her again. He knelt down and patted his back. "Hop on, Zo." He pointed toward the tree line, still no more than a bump on the horizon. "We're almost there. I can carry you the rest of the way."

Once she'd climbed up and wrapped her arms securely around his neck, he trudged on.

Every Zadarian knew you didn't leave a child behind. Only Bannari treated children as expendable, and Jeran was no Bannari.

In this example, we're clearly looking down on Jeran and his niece from the outside. We don't even know their names at first.

We don't feel what they're feeling inside. We're given evidence of what they might be feeling or thinking, but we only have one time when we're allowed to actually hear Jeran's thoughts.

This passage also doesn't have any flavor of Jeran's personality, and much of the language (like the word *qualms*) sounds like it belongs to someone other than a slave. We also hear some opinions of the narrator in sentences like "The gated communities were no place to raise a child."

Medium Narrative Distance

Now we're going to bring the passage closer. Jeran will be our POV character. We'll see through his eyes, but we won't be deep inside his viewpoint.

The morning sun beat down on the meadow, baking all the bushes into bare sticks and leaving nowhere for Jeran and Zoe to hide. Jeran glanced behind them and sighed. Their chances of escaping went down with every inch the

POINT OF VIEW | 93

sun rose in the sky, their travel speed cut in half by Zoe's smaller steps.

Stacie had begged him to take Zoe with him when he burrowed out. *She'll have a better chance out there,* Stacie said, *than in here slaving away for the Bannari.* True as her words were, now the extra responsibility weighed him down.

Zoe drooped against his side, half walking, half carried. He couldn't blame her. Neither of them had had any sleep the night before. But at the pace they were going, trackers would find them before they reached the cover of the trees, and sleeping out in the open was as good as handing themselves over to the trackers.

She stumbled and he steadied her again. He knelt down and patted his back. "Hop on, Zo." He pointed toward the tree line, still no more than a bump on the horizon. "We're almost there. I can carry you the rest of the way."

She climbed up and wrapped her arms around his neck, her grip threatening to cut off his ability to breathe.

He trudged on. They'd make it together or not at all. Every Zadarian knew you didn't leave a child behind. Only Bannari treated children as expendable, and Jeran was no Bannari.

We've come down inside Jeran. He uses their names because he knows them. He remembers Stacie's exact words to him. His word choices and less-formal sentence structure flavors the text. It feels more personal because we've come down from on high. But it's still not as close as we can go.

Close Narrative Distance

Now we're going to move close enough that we are Jeran, seeing what he sees, feeling what he feels, and hearing his voice.

Sweat trickled down Jeran's back, between his shoulder blades. The sun had melted the air into liquid, and every breath felt like he was drowning in a pot of teenan root soup. Except the soup tasted better than the air.

He glanced back at the seemingly empty meadow behind them. They should be able to spot trackers—the sun had burned away any bush cover—but that meant trackers could spot them, too. Their chances of escaping went down with every inch the sun rose in the sky. The guards had to know he and Zoe were gone by now.

Zoe drooped against his side, half walking, half carried. He couldn't blame her. Neither of them had any sleep the night before. But sleeping out in the open was as good as handing themselves over to the trackers. 'Course, at the pace they were going, trackers would find them before they reached the tree cover anyway.

You would have been able to travel faster without her, a voice in the back of his mind whispered. *You'd have had a better chance of escaping without her.*

Jeran shoved the voice away. Maybe he would have, but Stacie'd been right when she begged him to take Zoe with him. Better out than in, their father'd always said when someone tried to escape, even if they weren't certain what they'd find outside the walls. Even if attempting escape meant death.

Zoe stumbled and he steadied her again. He knelt down and patted his back. "Hop on, Zo." He pointed toward the tree line, still no more than a bump on the horizon. "We're almost there. I can carry you the rest of the way."

She climbed up and wrapped her arms around his neck. Her forearm crushed his Adam's apple, and pain dived down his neck. He looped his arms under her knees and shifted her up. The strangling pressure around his throat eased.

He trudged on. They'd make it together or not at all. Every Zadarian knew you didn't leave a child behind. Only

Bannari treated children as throwaway garbage, and Jeran was no Bannari.

Not only do we experience Jeran's internal, visceral reactions to things (the way his body reacts), but we feel the heat through him. It's no longer an abstract concept. We watch through his eyes as he interprets the world through what he has knowledge of and experience with.

The meadow is now "seemingly" empty because he can't be sure whether dangers hide in it.

His internal struggle over bringing Zoe with him is thrown into full emotional light. Part of him believes it was the right thing to do, and yet part of him wishes he didn't have the burden of her to care for, especially if it might cost him his chance at escape. We watch him make the decision not to abandon her.

This is Jeran's story now.

Telling

Now it's time to look at this passage told rather than shown. Pay attention to how this is different from the far narrative distance example. (You might want to flip back and read that one again quickly.)

> The morning sun was hot and had withered all the bushes and other groundcover, leaving runaways Jeran and Zoe nowhere to hide from the trackers who wanted to capture them and take them back to the gated community. Six-year-old Zoe drooped against his side. She was tired from being up all night and couldn't move as fast as he could, even at her best.
>
> His older sister, Stacie, had begged him to take Zoe with him when he escaped. The gated communities were a bad place to raise a child because they'd end up slaving their lives away for the Bannari.

But now, with Zoe slowing them down, he wondered if they'd even be able to make the tree line before they were caught. Maybe he should leave her behind.

Even as the thought entered his mind, he realized he could never leave her behind in order to save himself.

Zoe stumbled and he steadied her again. If they were going to make it, he'd have to carry her. The tree line was still miles away.

He knelt down and patted his back. "Hop on, Zo. We're almost there. I can carry you the rest of the way."

Once she'd climbed up and wrapped her arms securely around his neck, he trudged on.

Every Zadarian knew you didn't leave a child behind. Only Bannari treated children as expendable, and Jeran was no Bannari.

Compared to the previous versions, in this version there are a lot of explanations, very little personality to the voice (either from an omniscient narrator or from Jeran), and very little that you actually see playing out in real time in front of you on the page. Even in the far narrative distance example, we were watching things happen. We were watching from a distance, but we were still watching. In this version, the life has been stripped away.

AUTHOR INTRUSION AND THE FOURTH WALL

Now that you've seen how narrative distance works, I'll explain author intrusion and the fourth wall, because they're not the same as narrative distance.

Author intrusion and the fourth wall are two ways we either break the fictional dream or draw attention to the fact that the reader is reading a story. Because of this, they're easy to confuse, and that can be a problem because author intrusion damages our fiction, while breaking the fourth wall can be a strategic choice made to enhance our story.

In all types of fiction—books, plays, etc.—we have what's called a fourth wall. It's the invisible barrier between the characters and the reader. The characters don't know the reader exists. Whenever a character in the story or the story's narrator speaks directly to the reader, it breaks the fourth wall. This isn't always bad. In fact, many stories use it to good effect, but it is a strategically chosen technique.

I'll give you an example from television. Most television shows keep the fourth wall firmly in place. Everything happens as if no one is watching. The old TV sitcom *Saved By the Bell*, however, frequently broke that fourth wall. The character of Zack Morris would freeze time, talk to the viewer for a minute, and then the action would restart.

In books, this technique can be used in omniscient, in first-person, and in third-person POVs. Examples include Pseudonymous Bosch's *The Name of this Book Is Secret*, Brandon Sanderson's *Alcatraz Versus the Evil Librarians*, and Kurt Vonnegut's *Slaughterhouse-Five*. *Don Quixote* and *Jane Eyre* also fall into this category.

Whether or not you actually like this technique is a matter of personal preference. The key to breaking the fourth wall is to make it a conscious choice and to be consistent about it. We can't go through half the book with the fourth wall solidly intact and then break it and expect the reader to be alright with that. If we want to break the fourth wall, that break needs to be established early in the book so the reader knows this is how the book will treat the fourth wall.

Author intrusion is different. It happens any time an author who is supposed to be invisible makes their presence felt in the story. *Any time.*

I emphasize that because the common misunderstanding about author intrusion is that it only happens when the author of a first-person or third-person POV story includes a narrative paragraph full of political, religious, or socio-cultural commentary. (We'll look at whether author intrusion is possible in an omniscient story later, so for the rest of this section I'm talking only about first-person and third-person POVs.)

Author intrusion, at its foundational level, is simply another way of describing a point-of-view error.

Author intrusion includes when the author foretells what's coming in the future.

> George couldn't know how that simple meeting would change the course of his life.

> If Sandra had known that she was being watched, she would have locked the doors and pulled her blinds.

Author intrusion also includes when we give a character our personal opinion on a topic and allow them to pontificate on it, even if it doesn't fit the character or matter to the plot of the story. We've placed those opinions into the mouth and mind of a character where they don't belong.

On a small scale, author intrusion happens whenever we're in a close point of view and we use a word our character wouldn't use or give them knowledge about a topic (including terminology) that they wouldn't use.

The Fourth Wall vs. Author Intrusion in First-Person POV

In the chapter on first-person point of view, we looked at how first-person point-of-view books written in past tense have two options—either they treat the narrative as functionally the same as a third-person point-of-view story where the narrator isn't aware of the reader, or they're openly retrospective, where the first-person narrator is telling the story from some point in the future.

If our first-person story is retrospective, then we can, and probably will, break the fourth wall. If our first-person story isn't retrospective, then we have to be careful because breaking that fourth wall will count as a form of author intrusion. That first-person narrator isn't supposed to know the reader exists.

Figuring out if we've broken the fourth wall can sometimes be a challenge in first person because of the use of rhetorical questions.

> As long as I returned the money, it wasn't really stealing, right?

That type of question isn't meant to be answered and isn't really directed at anyone. It's the narrator basically talking to themselves—thinking. And that's what we have to ask ourselves to figure out whether we're breaking the fourth wall or not. Who is the narrator talking to?

A clue that our first-person narrator might be talking to the reader instead of to themselves is the use of *you*.

> You might define stealing a little differently, but to my way of thinking, as long as you put it back before anyone notices, you're really only borrowing.

Who is the narrator talking to here? The *you* means they're not talking to themselves anymore, but to someone else. We've broken the fourth wall.

The Fourth Wall vs. Author Intrusion in Omniscient POV

In omniscient point of view, the question of breaking the fourth wall vs. author intrusion comes down to whether the omniscient narrator is the author themselves or an all-knowing character they've created.

If the omniscient narrator is the author, then they can break the fourth wall (as long as they're consistent about it), and technically there's no such thing as author intrusion.

If the omniscient narrator is a constructed character, like Death in *The Book Thief*, then the author still has to stay true to that character. Anything that doesn't fit that character's perspective is, once again, author intrusion.

CHAPTER ELEVEN

Handling Stories with Multiple Viewpoint Characters

L IKE SO MANY WRITING CRAFT TOPICS, the selection of a viewpoint character is actually dual-pronged. The first question to answer is how many viewpoint characters we need for our story. The second question is, if we're going to have more than a single viewpoint character, how do we select the right one for each particular scene?

In this chapter, I'm going to look at the question of how many viewpoint characters we need and how to juggle multiple viewpoint characters. In the next chapter, I'll focus on selecting the right viewpoint character for a particular scene.

First, we need to go over the advantages and disadvantages of multiple viewpoint characters.

ADVANTAGES AND DISADVANTAGES OF MULTIPLE VIEWPOINT CHARACTERS

The main advantage of using multiple viewpoint characters is the breadth of scope it gives us. Using multiple viewpoint characters feels less claustrophobic because readers aren't restricted to the same head throughout the whole story. We can show different perspectives on the same event, allowing us to fully develop our theme. And we can show events and locations that a single viewpoint character wouldn't have access to. A well-done story with multiple viewpoint characters feels like life—only better, because we can see it from more perspectives than our own.

The disadvantages are a touch more varied. Multiple viewpoint characters can lead to subplots that don't matter and that distract from rather than enhance the main storyline. All our viewpoint characters' plotlines need to intersect at some point, either directly or indirectly contributing to the resolution of our story's core conflict.

Multiple viewpoint characters can also create a situation where the reader is trying to keep track of too many seemingly important characters and doesn't properly connect emotionally with any of them. Every time we include an additional viewpoint character, we're asking readers to invest in that character. It's a big commitment to either care about or hate each viewpoint character.

The flip side of this is that there's more for us, as authors, to keep track of. Multiple viewpoint characters create the need for multiple unique character voices. Not every writer has the ability or desire to create a wide range of voices.

Beyond this, to keep reader interest, every viewpoint character needs to be as interesting and compelling as all the others. Anyone who doesn't reach the standard set by the others can cause the reader to skim those scenes.

Finally, multiple viewpoint characters often means we're at risk of revealing too much to the reader. While it can be fun when the reader knows something our main character doesn't (a literary device known as dramatic irony), this can also swing too far in the other direction. If the reader knows everything each character is thinking and planning, the story can begin to feel stale because there's no room for suspense, misinterpretation, or discovering things at the same time as our main character.

QUESTIONS TO HELP MAKE THE DECISION

Despite the popularity of *Game of Thrones*, most of us don't need that many viewpoint characters to tell our stories. So how do we decide who to include and how many viewpoints to include?

I'll give you some questions to ask yourself. Some of these try to come at the same idea from different angles because looking at our problems or decisions from multiple sides can often give us a fresh perspective or break us out of a mental block. If you wanted to think about this another way, it's like trying to triangulate a location. Where the answers to these questions intersect will act as locators for your viewpoint character(s).

What are the conventions for our genre?

Take a look at the 10 most popular novels in your genre. How many viewpoint characters do they use? What roles do those characters play in the story? This can help guide us toward what our readers might expect. A good example is romance. The majority of romance novels will include scenes from the viewpoints of both characters involved in the relationship. If we're writing a romantic suspense, then the viewpoint characters might expand to include the villain.

What's the scope of our story?

This is somewhat related to your genre. An epic fantasy, spanning five planets where the fate of the galaxy is at stake, might require more viewpoint characters than the coming-of-age story of a young woman in feudal Japan. Generally speaking, the smaller the scope, the fewer the viewpoint characters we should use. The larger the scope, the more we can reasonably use, but that doesn't mean we must or should.

Which character has the most at stake over the course of the plot? Which character stands to make the biggest gain?

Answering these questions can help us decide which character is our protagonist. Our protagonist is the one we couldn't cut from the story without the story falling apart. Normally our protagonist will also be a viewpoint character.

Which character drives the plot? Which character has the strongest character arc (the growth or change a character undergoes during the course of the story)?

Similarly to the question above, the character driving the plot or the character who learns and grows the most over the course of the story are usually going to be the character or characters who should be viewpoint characters.

Does every potential viewpoint character influence the plot?

This is a good way to check that each potential viewpoint character is essential. If a character could be cut without having to change the plot in any significant way, or if another character could easily step in and take their place, they probably aren't a good choice for a viewpoint character because they're expendable.

Does including this viewpoint character's perspective enhance the theme?

Theme is always a tricky area for writers because we don't want readers to feel like we're beating them over the head with our message. Theme should develop through our main character's growth arc, but another way to enhance our theme is to have different characters approach it from varying angles and to take different sides on the issue. Those other characters don't necessarily need to be viewpoint characters, though, so what we want to look at is whether we need to be inside a character to truly understand their opinion and stance on the issue.

I'll give you an example. Say we're writing a mystery and we have a detective and her partner. The detective is our main character. She's the one driving our story. So do we also need scenes from the viewpoint of her partner? Maybe, maybe not.

If he's only there to be her sounding board, then we probably never need to go into his head. But, instead, if they're investigating a crime involving a local church and her partner is a devout Christian, then his perspective on the events and on the people involved would add new layers we couldn't develop if all we had was the viewpoint of our agnostic detective.

Which characters play a key role at the climax of the novel?

Our whole story builds up to the climax or the "final battle." The characters who are instrumental during this climax are the ones who are most important in the story. These are also good characters to consider for roles as viewpoint characters. If a character isn't involved in the climax of the story, then we need to seriously consider whether or not they deserve a role as a viewpoint character.

Would it add tension or otherwise improve the story to include scenes from the antagonist's viewpoint?

In some stories, we don't want to delve into the mind of our antagonist, either because the antagonist is an especially dark and twisted villain or because revealing the identity or plans of the antagonist would ruin the suspense and tension. In other stories, knowing the antagonist and his or her plans increases the tension as readers worry about whether our heroes will spot the trap in time.

Does every viewpoint character we're considering have a strong reason for being a viewpoint character?

Each viewpoint character we include needs to have goals, motivations, and stakes within the story and to give a valuable perspective on the situation. This guideline is a major determiner for whether or not a viewpoint character's scenes work.

If we're only considering giving a potential viewpoint character one or two scenes, then this is a clue that maybe they shouldn't be a viewpoint character. This usually means we want to make this person a viewpoint character to shoehorn in information or to show a part of the story that probably doesn't need to be shown.

DANGERS TO AVOID

Even after answering all those questions, we might still end up vacillating over whether or not to give a particular character some scenes in their viewpoint. That's because there are no hard rules when it comes to selecting viewpoint characters. There are only guidelines that can help us make the best choices.

In this section, I'm going to quickly delve into some of the red flags that should warn us off from giving a character scenes in their viewpoint. These reasons for wanting to make someone a viewpoint character aren't good enough reasons to do so.

To info dump or include backstory.

If we're considering adding a viewpoint character simply to be able to include backstory, this isn't a good enough reason. Backstory that's truly important to the story should come out naturally through the course of the story. When we create a viewpoint character because that's the only way to share that backstory, it probably means this is something the reader doesn't need to know. We shouldn't include backstory simply because we like it or find it interesting.

The same holds true for information dumps. We shouldn't make someone a viewpoint character simply to be able to tell the reader something. For example, we shouldn't create a viewpoint character who is fascinated with volcanoes simply so that they can muse about volcanoes, thereby educating the reader. We also shouldn't create a character who knows nothing about volcanoes for the sole purpose of having them need to ask questions and thereby educate the reader about volcanoes. On their own, those aren't good enough reasons to make someone a viewpoint character.

To show something our other viewpoint characters aren't aware of.

If we're considering adding a viewpoint character simply because we want to include a scene that our main character can't be present at, this isn't a good enough reason. I most often see this in my editing work when the main character is knocked unconscious or is otherwise so ill that they can't serve as the eyes for the story. Writers will sometimes create a temporary viewpoint character to serve as the story's eyes while the main character is incapacitated. We don't need to do this. It's usually more interesting for the reader to worry about what's happening and to be caught up later, along with the main character.

If we want to add a viewpoint character to show parts of the story that can't be told any other way, we need to make sure that character also exists for a bigger reason within the story. Are they a well-rounded character in their own right, with goals and stakes of their own? Are their scenes interesting enough that a reader won't skim them? Do they add something valuable to the story?

To show something that doesn't affect the protagonist at all.

Our story might have multiple viewpoint characters and multiple main characters, but the story belongs to one character—the protagonist. Even in a romance, one character is usually the one driving the plot or with the most at stake. So everything we show should affect the protagonist and their story goal in some way.

To explain something that will otherwise seem like a coincidence, like a contrivance, or like *deus ex machina*.

This usually indicates a larger problem with our plot. The solution isn't to drop in a viewpoint character that has no other reason for being a viewpoint character than to fix it. The solution is to objectively look at our plot and fix the problem organically, in a way that will make sense without having to stick in a new viewpoint character.

(*Deus ex machina* is a plot contrivance where a seemingly hopeless situation is solved by help from an unexpected source.)

TIPS FOR USING MULTIPLE VIEWPOINT CHARACTERS

For those of us who've decided we do want to use multiple viewpoint characters, the next question becomes how to manage them in the best possible way.

When we switch viewpoint characters, make the switch clear in the very first sentence of the new scene/chapter.

One of the biggest risks with multiple viewpoint characters is confusing the reader. Any time we confuse the reader, any time they have to pause in their reading to figure out what's happening, they're jerked out of the fictional dream and they lose connection to the story. That makes it much easier for them to put the book down and go do something else.

The reader needs to know immediately whose head they're in after a scene or chapter break. This is true even if we don't switch POV characters during the break. When the new scene or chapter opens, we need to let the reader know they're still inside the same viewpoint character.

A quick and easy way to do this is to combine an external action by the viewpoint character with something internal in the viewpoint character, whether that be internal dialogue or an internal visceral reaction. That gives the reader a chance to settle in, and then we can continue with the rest of the scene.

Switch viewpoint characters strategically and show or hint at the reason for the switch.

Please remember that, when I say "switch viewpoint characters," I always mean "switch viewpoint characters using a proper transition."

In the next chapter, we'll spend more time on how to select the right viewpoint character for each scene, but the guiding principle when we make a viewpoint switch is that it should be something the reader will want. That's a vague way of saying it, though, so I'll give some examples.

We might switch viewpoints when one viewpoint character has put another character into conflict, either internally or externally, and we want to experience that conflict through the eyes of the character experiencing it. We might change viewpoints when we want to highlight the contradictions in the way two characters view the same event. We might change viewpoints if one character's goals or stakes will better fit the next step in the story.

Make sure our timelines synch up.

This holds true even if your story isn't laid out chronologically (for example, in a non-linear narrative like *Eternal Sunshine of the Spotless Mind*). When Character A and Character B show up in the same scene, you need to make sure they're on the same day—you don't want Character A to be on Monday in their timeline while Character B is on Wednesday in theirs.

Don't show the same event from two different points of view.

It's often useful to show the differing interpretations of an event by two viewpoint characters or to show both of their reactions to the same event. However, you don't want to travel the same ground multiple times. We don't need to see the car crash scene from Mary's point of view and then again from Bob's point of view. Even when we're showing interpretations of or reactions to the same thing, it still needs to be done in such a way that the story moves forward, rather than staying in the same place, like our characters are running on a timewarp treadmill.

Understand how all the strands of our story braid together and influence each other.

What I mean by this is that, even if our viewpoint characters aren't together in a scene—maybe aren't even on the same continent or in the same era—we need to know how what one character does in this particular scene will affect all the other characters.

In chaos theory, this is known as the butterfly effect. A small change in an earlier condition can create a very different result later on in the timeline. (The term was coined by mathematician Edward Lorenz, who was creating weather models and gave the metaphorical example of how the path and intensity of a hurricane could be changed by something as small as the flapping of a butterfly's wings.)

In fiction, it means that a small action of one character in a different time or place can still radically change the trajectory another character's life will take. Understanding this butterfly effect in fiction is how we, as authors, create the feeling of a real, interconnected, dynamic world.

When we're writing a single viewpoint character, this doesn't come into play in the same way. Our secondary characters are still acting off-screen, but our experience of that is limited. We only experience what our single viewpoint character experiences, and therefore, we're always thinking in terms of how events affect that character and we only show the ones that do. We don't independently see the events that lead up to that effect.

Think beyond the current viewpoint character when multiple viewpoint characters are together in a scene.

We can start to trip over terms here, so to explain this clearly, I'm going to use an example of a story where we have two characters that each have scenes from their point of view. We'll call them Meagan and Bob.

If we have Meagan and Bob in the same scene, we need to keep both of their goals and emotions in mind, even though only Meagan's side will make it onto the page at that moment if she's our current viewpoint character.

This creates continuity in the storyline and character arcs even when you're moving back and forth between viewpoints. If we don't keep our other viewpoint characters in mind, when we swap back to the other viewpoint, it can sometimes feel like the events of the previous scene didn't matter. They should matter.

For example, say we're in Meagan's point of view and she reveals something personal to Bob. That personal revelation should now influence Bob's emotions, opinions, and actions when we return to his point of view. If he moves forward as if that revelation never happened, it's going to feel inauthentic and strange to the reader, as if there's a disconnect. Even if Bob pretends outwardly that Meagan never revealed her secret, inside it matters.

This is different from a story with a single viewpoint character because, even though all our other characters still have their own goals and emotions, we'll only experience them through our viewpoint character and never from inside those other characters themselves. In other words, there is forced continuity.

> **Additional Tip:** If you're struggling to figure out how to have your non-viewpoint character react believably in a scene, switch your perspective. Consider the scene as if you were inside the non-viewpoint character. Head-hop if you need to and then delete the head-hopping segments from the scene afterward.

Create conflict while still forcing them to work together.

In a book where our viewpoint characters are together more than they're apart and where they're working toward the same collective goal, we can easily run into one of two problems.

The first is where there's no conflict between our viewpoint characters. The second is where there's too much conflict—they're constantly fighting or insulting each other without a clear reason for it because the author realizes stories where everyone gets along are boring. The first is boring. But the second is annoying and feels juvenile. It can also make one or both of the characters come across as unlikeable.

We need to find ways to avoid both problems.

Solution #1 – Give them a conflict apart from the goal they're both working toward. For example, in Lindsay Buroker's *Balanced on the Blades Edge*, Sardelle is secretly a magic user and Ridge is prejudiced against magic users and, as a military colonel, would be obligated to turn her over for execution if he found out her true nature.

Solution #2 – Give them differing ideas about the best way to reach their common goal. For example, one character might be willing to sacrifice something (either physical objects or moral lines) that the other character isn't willing to bend on or lose.

Solution #3 – Have them want the same thing but for different reasons. For example, our characters are a treasure hunter and an archeologist. Both want to reach the tomb where—legend has it—the real Excalibur is hidden. But one wants to put the sword in a museum and the other wants to sell it for profit. The key to this solution is to make each motivation essential for the character it belongs to and to make the stakes high for both.

Make sure our protagonist receives the biggest percentage of viewpoint scenes.

This is supposed to be their story, after all. If we find ourselves wanting to give more scenes to someone who isn't the protagonist, we need to ask ourselves why. Is that character more compelling in some way? If so, then we need to either fix our protagonist or consider changing our protagonist.

Even when our protagonist isn't the viewpoint character, remember that this is still their story. If possible, it's a good idea for our current viewpoint character to think about our protagonist, even if they aren't around.

In the next chapter, we'll talk more about finding the right balance of scenes between viewpoint characters.

CHAPTER TWELVE

Choosing Your Viewpoint Character(s)

I F YOU HAVE ONLY A SINGLE VIEWPOINT character for your story, or if you're writing in omniscient point of view, then you already know whose viewpoint you'll be using. For everyone else, each scene requires a choice—who will this scene belong to?

Sometimes we'll instinctively know who our viewpoint character should be for a scene. When that's not the case, here are some questions we can ask to help us figure it out.

As I've done before, I've grouped similar questions together because, taken together, they can help us narrow down our possibilities by helping us look at the same issue from different angles.

Which character has the most at stake (either to gain or to lose)?

Who will take the biggest risks? Who will suffer the most if the goal fails? Who is the most invested in the goal?

High stakes mean high interest in the reader. The more we show how invested our character is in something, the more our reader will become invested as well.

You'll often hear the advice that the viewpoint character should always be the character that has the most to lose in a scene, the one with the most at stake. While that's definitely a criterion in selecting our viewpoint character, it shouldn't be the only one.

Who does the scene focus on?

This is another way of asking "who is the most important person in this scene?"

Whose goal drives the scene?

Knowing whose goal drives the scene doesn't necessarily mean this is the viewpoint character we want to choose.

We might because it's implicitly interesting to see a character struggle to achieve something they want to achieve.

We might not because perhaps we want to show what another character thinks about this goal. It can also be interesting to see through the eyes of a character who believes the goal is foolhardy or worthless and then see if they're proven right or wrong and how they feel about that.

Which character has the highest emotional investment in the scene?

Another way of saying this is "who cares about the outcome the most?"

We can also sometimes think about this in terms of rising and falling. Whose emotional state will change the most over the course of the scene?

Which character will have an epiphany in this scene?

This could be a character that finally puts all the pieces together and solves a key problem or puzzle the characters have been facing. It could also be a character that has an emotional epiphany at a turning point.

When a character makes a step forward on their growth arc, we normally need to show that from inside the character in order for the reader to find it believable (and also because the reader will usually *want* to see it from the inside).

Which character's motivations and goals need to be made clearer?

Many factors go into believability in fiction, but a major element is whether our viewpoint character believes strongly enough in something and whether the reader understands why they believe a certain course of action is the best/only one. The more of a stretch a character's goal or motivation is, the more time we need to spend developing it in order for the reader to go along with us.

Which character's perspective will be the most interesting or relatable?

This might not immediately sound like a strategic choice, but it can influence our choice more than it would seem at first.

For example, perhaps we need a character to act in a way that our readers won't be able to relate to (or won't want to relate to) because of the depth of the pettiness or selfishness involved. We might want to show that scene from a different viewpoint and then only return to the un-relatable character when they're regretting their action.

Also, the most interesting character might not be the one with the most at stake (as we talked about above). It might be the one who has the most interesting perspective on what's happening. In some scenes, it might be better to choose the character with the unique perspective over the character with the most at stake.

How do we want the events presented to the reader?

Each of our viewpoint characters should be a unique individual. The way they see the world around them should be different from the way anyone else sees the world. They are judging and interpreting what happens in the story.

So when we're trying to decide who should be the viewpoint character for any scene, we have to ask ourselves how we want the events of this scene portrayed to the reader. What tone do we want? What perspective do we want given on the events?

For example, let's say we have viewpoint character that is a Marine Corps captain who has dedicated his life to protecting his country and who has done three combat deployments. In the same story, we also have a viewpoint character that is a pacifist who believes that there's no justifiable reason to go to war. The same event will be portrayed very differently through the eyes of one compared to the other.

Or, if we have an optimistic, hopeful character, the tone she conveys in a scene will be different from the tone a more pessimistic, cynical character will give to the scene.

Whose eyes we view the scene through will influence the tone of the scene and the spin given to the events in it.

What emotions do we want the reader to experience?

We want the reader to feel like our story is real. We want to be invisible. But, at the same time, we are in control. This is our creation. So for each scene, we should ask ourselves what emotion we want to evoke in the reader.

For example, say we have a book where a child has been kidnapped. The emotion conveyed to the reader will be different depending on whether we show a scene through the eyes of the distraught mother who lost her husband in a car accident three months before compared to showing it through the eyes of the hardened FBI agent called in to work the case.

Is there a detail that the reader needs to know for the story to make sense?

Sometimes every potential viewpoint character will have the same knowledge, but not always. Sometimes the characters will each possess different levels of knowledge about the events.

But this consideration has another layer to it. We might need a character to notice a particular detail that will be important later on in the story. Not every possible viewpoint character might notice that essential detail. If we want the reader to know about it now, so that it's foreshadowed in a subtle way for later, we need to select the viewpoint character who would notice that detail.

Think about it this way. When you walk into the room, do you notice the exact same things about that room as your spouse or your child or your mother would notice? When my mom walks into a room, she'll notice if it's dirty or cluttered. I won't. I will notice any smells and I'll be drawn to any pictures that are on the walls.

A lot of what we talked about earlier in terms of maintaining a consistent point of view dealt with making sure that we only share what the viewpoint character would notice. This begins with the selection of the strategically best viewpoint character for the scene.

If we need to withhold something from the reader, which character isn't privy to that information (or knows the least)?

In *The Princess Bride*, there's a scene where Westley (still known to Buttercup as the Dread Pirate Roberts) engages in a battle of wits with Sicilian criminal genius Vizzini. Westley says he'll put iocaine powder (a deadly poison) into one of the goblets of wine, and they'll both drink. When Westley isn't looking, Vizzini switches their cups. They drink and Vizzini dies. We learn afterward that Westley poisoned both cups because he has built up an immunity to iocaine powder.

The scene works because, while the battle of wits is taking place, we don't know Westley has an immunity to iocaine powder. Had we seen this scene through Westley's eyes, that fact would have had to be revealed to the reader, and it would have stripped the scene of all its tension. We'd have had nothing to worry about as readers.

Do this with a light hand. If you use this technique too often, the reader will end up feeling cheated or manipulated, and that's not good.

What character knows the least about something we want the reader to learn?

This is the opposite of the question above. Sometimes we have information the reader needs to know, and we have to find a natural, believable way to give it to them. A character who also doesn't yet know this information can be a great solution because the reader will learn along with them. This character acts as the conduit—they wonder about the situation and ask the questions the reader will also be asking themselves. As I mentioned earlier, though, we shouldn't create a viewpoint character solely for this purpose. They should also have other reasons that qualify them for the role.

DO ALL OUR VIEWPOINT CHARACTERS NEED TO HAVE THE SAME NUMBER OF SCENES?

Since we're talking about selecting viewpoint characters, this is the next natural question.

The simple answer is *no*. The more complex answer is that it depends on who our viewpoint characters are and their role in the story.

The number of scenes and the relative percentage of scenes a character receives depend on their importance to the story.

If we have two main characters, for example, then we'll often want to keep their scenes as even as possible. (This is regularly the case within the romance genre because romance writers will have both members of the relationship as viewpoint characters.)

But the more scenes we give a character, the more important the reader will consider them. Because of this, we don't need to balance the number of scenes belonging to secondary characters or to the antagonist. In fact, we shouldn't give them as many scenes as our main character(s). In everything we write, we need to remember who the story belongs to.

CHAPTER THIRTEEN

Take It to the Page
Practical Application

I N EACH OF MY BUSY WRITER'S GUIDES, I LIKE
to include checklists, questions, or other editing helps to make it
easier for you to apply what you've learned to your own project.
These Take It to the Page exercises look a little different in each
book because I customize them to the topic at hand. For POV, I've
brought them together in one chapter.

I've done this for a few reasons. The first is that not every chapter in this particular book required a Take It to the Page section at
the end. The second is that this allows you to have all the helps in
one place, and quickly skim to the ones you need at the time you
need them, rather than trying to remember which chapter they were
attached to a few months down the road when you might want to
switch points of view or might need help figuring out which viewpoint character is the right one for the scene you're struggling with.

The third is that many of the concepts couldn't be accurately applied until you'd read multiple chapters (for example, comparing omniscient POV with head-hopping in your writing).

Keep in mind as you go through these exercises that they won't solve all the potential point-of-view issues your book might have. Point of view is pervasive. It colors everything, and the only way to catch all the possible errors is through a slow and careful read of our book. That said, there are still some things we can do to speed up the process. In the following exercises, you'll find ways to streamline and catch a large portion of potential problems.

CHOOSING THE RIGHT POINT OF VIEW FOR YOUR STORY

By now you probably already know which point of view you want to use for your story, but I'm going to quickly give you some questions you can ask yourself anyway. These are great if you're unsure or if you just want to double-check that you have, in fact, chosen the best option for you and the story you want to tell.

Question 1 – What point of view is the norm for your genre? Don't let this be the final determiner, but it's important to know what readers will be expecting. And completely ignore what you think sells—those trends change all the time.

Question 2 – What type of POV do you most enjoy reading? If you're not sure, quickly list your five favorite books and the two books you've most enjoyed this year. What POV are they written in?

Question 3 – What type comes more naturally to you? If you're not sure, try writing a single scene more than once, changing it based on the point of view.

Question 4 – What level of distance do you want your reader to feel?

Question 5 – Does your particular plot dictate a certain type?

IMPROVING YOUR OMNISCIENT POINT-OF-VIEW STORY

These questions (and the ones for first-person POV) assume you've already read the chapter on omniscient POV and that you understand the theory behind the questions. If you haven't yet read the chapters associated with these questions, I strongly recommend you do so first.

Step 1 – Have you chosen to break the fourth wall anywhere in your book? If so, have you established this within the first two chapters? Have you followed up by regularly reminding the reader that the fourth wall has been broken? (If you go for a quarter of the book without speaking directly to the reader, it can feel jarring when you break the fourth wall again.)

Step 2 – If you're short on time, take two to three chapters and run a check for head-hopping. If you have time, run this check for your whole book.

Check each scene. Have you shown the thoughts or other internalizations for more than one character per scene? If not, you're fine. If so, make sure that you've maintained the voice of your omniscient narrator rather than using the voice and personality of the character.

Step 3 – Are you telling rather than writing in a vibrant, far-narrative distance?

Telling is too big a topic for me to give you all the checks here (since I also haven't discussed all the nuances of telling in this book). If you want more checks, please see my book *Showing and Telling in Fiction*. I will, however, give you a spot to start.

<u>Part A</u> – Search for the words in the following list. Have you used these words to tell the reader that one of your characters is thinking, rather than showing *what* the character is thinking or instead of implying it through their actions? (Remember, in omnisci-

ent, we won't always hear the exact thoughts of all the characters. We'll only share the most important ones.)

realized

wondered

thought

knew

remembered

recalled

reviewed

considered

Part B – Go through each chapter and read the passages where you've described something. Highlight any adjectives—words that modify nouns or pronouns. Examples of adjectives include *amazing*, *scary*, *big*, and *hot*. Have you generalized in your description? Can you make your description more specific to give the reader a clearer picture?

Part C – If you have a word processing program (like Microsoft Word 2010 or newer) that will highlight every instance of a word that you search for, run a search for the words *is*, *was*, and *were*. For each result, ask yourself the following questions.

Am I reporting a fact? (E.g., "She was ugly.") If so, how could I give evidence instead? What carefully selected details would best lead readers to the correct conclusion? Is the detail I've chosen to use consistent with what my point-of-view character would notice?

Helping and state-of-being verbs can often be replaced by stronger, tighter verbs. For example...

Emily was walking to work.

Becomes...

Emily walked to work.

Can the helping or state-of-being verbs you've located be removed to make your writing tighter and stronger?

Part D – Run a search for the word *because*. Have you used it to explain motivation?

IMPROVING YOUR FIRST-PERSON-POINT-OF-VIEW STORY

These questions assume that you've read the chapter on first-person POV and understand the theory and challenges of this perspective. If you haven't yet read the chapter on first-person POV, I strongly recommend you do that first.

Step 1 – Is your first-person story retrospective?

- If so, why is your narrator telling this story? Has this influenced what you've shown and what you've withheld?

- If so, is your narrator unreliable? Have you planted at least three subtle hints that your narrator might not be able to be trusted?

Step 2 – Have you created a unique character voice? Ask yourself the following questions about your main character.

- How do they view the world around them? (E.g., mostly evil, mostly good, fair, unfair, random, ordered by a bigger plan...)

- How do they view themselves?

- How do they feel about the big-ticket items like love and faith?

- How do they feel about the people closest to them?

- Are they cynical or optimistic?

Now try to think of at least one place where these elements show themselves on the actual pages of your story. (They don't all need to show up, but if you don't put it on the page, the reader can't know it.) Their voice should color how they interpret the world around them, so if you can't find examples, it could indicate a problem.

Step 3 – Use the Find and Replace feature in Microsoft Word (or whatever word processing program you're using) to highlight all the uses of *I*.

To do this in MS Word, you hit the More option in the Find and Replace box. This will allow you to select Match Case and Find Whole Words Only. (Those are essential or you'll have a bunch of false results because it will pull out every *i* in every word.) Type *I* in the Find What box. Then move your cursor to the Replace With box. Once you see it blinking there, you'll need to click on the option for Format at the bottom of the box. Within the pop-up window, you can choose whether you want to change all instances of *I* to a different color, bold, a different size, or all of those. The key is to make them stand out. (You can use the same process in reverse to change it back to normal after.)

Hit Okay in that secondary box, and then Replace All in the main Find and Replace box. Now you'll be able to easily see how many times you use *I* and in what pattern. Ask yourself the following questions.

- Do most of my sentences begin with *I*?
- If so, is it because I haven't added enough variety to my sentences? Add more variety.
- If so, do many of these *I* sentences pair up with state-of-being verbs like *was* or *have*? Do many of these sentences also use the words *to* and *for*? Both of these are signs that you might not be showing us what the narrator is doing and feeling. Check these sentences to see if you're

telling us what she did and felt or what she planned to do rather than showing it.

Step 4 – Have you written in scenes?

Step 5 – Have you alternated internal with external so the story doesn't feel claustrophobic? A good way to check this is to use your word processing program to highlight internal passages in one color and external passages in another so you can see the pattern. If you're in a rush, do this on one or two scenes. This will show you if you have a problem with this. If you have time, go through your whole book for the thorough treatment.

Step 6 – Does your first-person narrator come across as stupid? Because we're not always objective about our own stories, this is a good question to pose to our beta readers, critique group, or editor. If you have a scene that you think might be a problem, talk it through with one of these people or even a non-writer friend, or show it to them.

Step 7 – Are you writing in present tense or have you written a first-person past-tense story that you're treating functionally the same as a third-person story? If so, check that you haven't broken the fourth wall. You can use the same Find and Replace process as you used to search for *I*, but this time search for *you*. (Don't select Match Case since this time you want both *You* and *you*.) Ignore any time *you* shows up in dialogue. Does it show up anywhere else? If so, you might be breaking the fourth wall.

CHECKING FOR POINT-OF-VIEW ERRORS

Point-of-view errors are so subtle that we can't catch all of them with a few tricks or checks. We'll only catch them by carefully reading our book, keeping in mind as we go who the current scene belongs to. What I can do, though, is give you a few tools that will at least help you clean up some of them and make the process quicker.

Step 1 – Run a search for titles and relational names (e.g., sister, brother, teacher, doctor) that you might have used in your book. Check each of these to see if they represent a POV error.

Step 2 – Think about your book. Have you potentially called a character by different names throughout the book? Decide on what you'd like this character to be called (or what they'll be consistently called by each other character during that character's viewpoint scenes) and use the Find feature in your word processing program to locate the variations that you need to change. If you plan to use only one name for the character, you can use Find and Replace to speed up the process of making name usage consistent. (You might do this if you have only one viewpoint character or if all your viewpoint characters would refer to this person in the same way.)

Step 3 – If you've already worked through the practical exercises in my book *Showing and Telling in Fiction*, then this step might look familiar. It also might seem long, but it's going to help you fix telling in your viewpoint character at the same time as you catch point-of-view errors. One of the ways to be efficient with our time is to take care of two potential issues at once.

Run a search for the emotion-themed words in the following list. These are by no means the only words for emotions, but they'll help you catch the most common ones. (You might also want to try variations on the word or try typing in the root of the word—for example, type in *sad*, not *sadness*, because a search for *sad* will show you *sad*, *sadness*, *sadly*, etc. as long as you *don't* select "Whole Words Only.")

If this emotion is attributed to your viewpoint character, are you naming the emotion the character is feeling? Figure out your character's root emotion, the nuances of it, and why they're feeling it, and then create a fresh way to show that emotion to the reader.

If this emotion is attributed to a non-viewpoint character, use one of the guiding principles explained in Chapter Nine to fix the point-of-view error.

afraid
agitated
alarmed
amazed
amused
angry
anguish
annoyed
anxious
ashamed
bitter
bored
calm
cautious
cheerful
comfortable
compassion
concerned
confident
confused
contempt
curious
defeated
defensive
depressed
desperate
determined

disappointed

disgusted

disillusioned

dismayed

disoriented

distrust

doubtful

dread

eager

embarrassed

enthusiastic

envious

excited

exhausted

frustrated

grateful

grief

grumpy

guilty

happy

hateful

helpless

hesitant

hopeful/hopeless

horrified

hostile

humiliated

hurt

impatient

indifferent

insecure

insulted

interested

irritated

jealous

joyful

lonely

mad

nervous

nostalgic

numb

optimistic

outraged

overwhelmed

panic

paranoid

pity

proud

rage

regretful

rejected

relaxed

relieved

reluctant

remorseful

resentful

resigned

restless

revulsion

sad

satisfied

scornful

self-conscious

shame

shocked

skeptical

smug

sorrowful

spiteful

stressed

stunned

surprised

suspicious

sympathetic

tired

uncomfortable

vengeful

wary

weary

worried

Step 4 – POV errors involving motivations are one of the more difficult instances of telling to catch because there's no easy way to use the Search or Find features of your word processing program. Read through the chapter you're working on and look specifically for instances where your character does one thing **to** do something else. (E.g., "She grabbed her bow **to** shoot the deer.") Change each of these spots so that your character performs the two actions. (E.g., "She grabbed her bow **and** shot the deer.")

Step 5 – Search for the words in the following list. Have you used these words to tell the reader that a non-viewpoint character is thinking or noticing something? (If you want to use this step to save yourself time later, have you used these words to tell the reader what your viewpoint character is thinking, rather than showing them think it?)

noticed

realized

wondered

thought

knew

remembered

recalled

reviewed

considered

Step 6 – Run a search for the following words/phrases. Have you used them to break POV? If so, rewrite the passage.

unknowingly

didn't notice

unconsciously

unaware

Step 7 – In this step, you're going to try to find places where you've created a POV error by violating the temporal order.

Use the Find and Replace feature in your word processing program this time. Here's what you should enter.

Find: as

Replace: AS

(Make sure you put a space in front of and behind "as" or that you select "Whole Words Only" otherwise your search will show you every time an *a* appears next to an *s*.

By replacing the smaller case *as* with all caps, they'll jump out at you.

For every AS, ask yourself the following questions.

- Have you reversed cause and effect? If so, make sure you have the action come first, followed by the reaction.
- Have you created a situation where two things are grammatically happening at the same time that can't actually happen at the same time? Rewrite it as two separate sentences to show the real sequence of events.

For any *as* that serves a legitimate purpose in the sentence, simply change it back to the lowercase.

Repeat this process for *when* and *while.*

QUESTIONS TO HELP YOU DECIDE HOW MANY VIEWPOINT CHARACTERS TO USE

Part of the purpose of these questions is to make sure that we've thought through our decisions and have good reasons for making the choices we make. Then, even if we decide to go against conventional advice, we can have more confidence that we're making the best choice for our story.

Question 1 – What are the conventions for your genre?

Question 2 – What's the scope of your story?

Question 3 – Which character has the most at stake over the course of the plot? Which character stands to make the biggest gain?

Question 4 – Which character drives the plot? Which character has the strongest character arc (the growth or change a character undergoes during the course of the story)?

Question 5 – Does every potential viewpoint character influence the plot?

Question 6 – Does including this viewpoint character's perspective enhance the theme?

Question 7 – Which character(s) play a key role at the climax of the novel?

Question 8 – Would it add tension or otherwise improve the story to include scenes from the antagonist's viewpoint?

Question 9 – Does every viewpoint character you're considering have a strong reason for being a viewpoint character?

EDITING CHECKS FOR YOUR MULTIPLE-VIEWPOINT-CHARACTER STORY

Before diving in to these checks, remember that omniscient POV stories don't have multiple viewpoint characters. They have a single viewpoint—that of the narrator. For this reason, none of these steps apply to omniscient POV stories.

Step 1 – Read over two to three chapters. Have you used a proper transition each time you've switched viewpoints? If not, rewrite the chapter to use proper transitions. If you find many times when you've switched without a proper transition, this is a clue that you probably struggle with head-hopping and should do this check for the remainder of your book.

Step 2 – For each scene, is the viewpoint character clear within the first sentence? If not, rewrite the opening sentences to make the viewpoint character immediately clear.

Step 3 – When you switch viewpoint characters between scenes, ask yourself the following questions:

- Do I have a good reason for switching viewpoint characters at this point? (If you're not sure, go to the Questions to Help You Choose the Right Viewpoint Character section.)

- Have I shown or hinted at the reason for the switch?

Step 4 – For scenes where you have two viewpoint characters together in the same place, ask yourself the following questions:

- Have I stayed consistent to the perspective of only one of these characters throughout the scene? If so, good. If not, fix the head-hopping.
- Do the timelines for each character match up? (E.g., they're both on Wednesday in their own timelines.)
- Are my other characters acting consistent to their personalities throughout the scene? (In other words, they should be more than props for the current viewpoint character.)
- Does what happens in this scene affect the emotions and thoughts of my other viewpoint characters in the following scenes?

Step 5 – Skim through your book. Have you shown the same event from two different viewpoints? If so, decide which viewpoint is best for conveying what you want to convey in this scene. Remove the other scene. If you have essential elements that will be lost in this deletion, find other places where you can insert them. Remember, each scene is supposed to move the story forward, rather than covering ground we've already covered.

Step 6 – Jot down all the plot threads in your book. Do they all eventually intersect in some way? How do they influence each other? If you find a thread that doesn't relate to the others in some way, consider deleting it or altering it so it influences or is influenced by other parts of the plot.

QUESTIONS TO HELP YOU CHOOSE THE RIGHT VIEWPOINT CHARACTER

You can use these questions either during the outlining/drafting stage if you're struggling to figure out which character should own the scene. You can also use these questions after finishing your first draft if you find a scene that doesn't seem quite right. Sometimes the problem ends up being that you've selected the wrong viewpoint character.

Question 1 – Which character has the most at stake (either to gain or to lose)?

Question 2 – Who does the scene focus on?

Question 3 – Whose goal drives the scene?

Question 4 – Which character has the highest emotional investment in the scene?

Question 5 – Which character will have an epiphany in this scene?

Question 6 – Which character's motivations and goals need to be made clearer?

Question 7 – Which character's perspective will be the most interesting or relatable?

Question 8 – How do we want the events presented to the reader?

Question 9 – What emotions do we want the reader to experience?

Question 10 – Is there a detail that the reader needs to know for the story to make sense? Who knows it or notices it?

Question 11 – If we need to withhold something from the reader, which character isn't privy to that information (or knows the least)?

Question 12 – What character knows the least about something we want the reader to learn?

HOW TO BALANCE SCENES AMONG VIEWPOINT CHARACTERS

In Chapter Eleven, we talked about the need to balance the number of scenes our viewpoint characters have. Our protagonist needs to own the majority of scenes because this is their story. However, if we have multiple main characters, their viewpoint scenes should also be relatively equal.

Complete the following checks to make sure your scenes are balanced the way they need to be.

Check 1 – How many scenes does each viewpoint character have? Does your protagonist "own" the majority? If you have two main characters, are their numbers approximately balanced? (They don't need to be exactly the same, but they should normally be close.)

Using Microsoft Word – If you're using MS Word (or another standard word processing program), skim through your file and simply keep a running tally of how many scenes belong to each viewpoint character.

Using Scrivener – Scrivener allows you to add General Meta-Data to each of your scenes/chapters. A quick way to check for balance is to set your Label field to Point of View, and then choose a different color for each viewpoint character. This allows you to use the corkboard or the outliner to quickly count the number of scenes belonging to each viewpoint character.

Check 2 – What's the total word count of all the scenes devoted to each viewpoint character? Your protagonist should have more words devoted to their scenes than any other viewpoint character has individually. Also, you'll normally want more words devoted to your protagonist's scenes than to the other viewpoint characters' scenes combined. If you have two main characters, check to see if their word counts are approximately equal.

Using Microsoft Word – If you're using MS Word, the quickest way to check the word count is to create separate files for each viewpoint character. Copy and paste their scenes into that file. Word will then show you the total word count for each file.

Using Scrivener – If you labeled your scenes/chapters in the previous check, then this becomes very simple. Use the Search bar to search in Point of View. Now enter a viewpoint character's name. Scrivener will bring up their scenes. Once it does, select all those scenes from the Search Results at the left of the screen. Then, go to the Project menu and select Text Statistics. This will give you the word count for only the selected scenes. (If that sounds too complicated, run the search, and then use the outliner view. It will show you the word count of each scene and you can add them up with a calculator.)

Please note that I have the Windows version of Scrivener. If you have the Mac version, how you do this might be slightly different.

Check 3 – If you have two main characters (who are viewpoint characters), have you alternated between them relatively evenly? You don't need to create a perfect back-and-forth pattern, but if you go too long (more than a few scenes) without switching, it can lead to the reader feeling disconnected from the neglected main character. It can also indicate a problem with your plot. Perhaps the neglected character isn't a main character after all.

Using Microsoft Word – This is the most time-intensive check. You'll need to use a new file to write out a quick scene list. You don't have to include any of the details of each scene. All that matters is who the scene belongs to. To make it easier, I recommend that you write each character's name in a different color as you add their name to the list.

Using Scrivener – As long as you've labeled each scene/chapter with the viewpoint character and have given each a different color, you can quickly see whether you're alternating evenly using the corkboard or outliner view.

Other Books by Marcy Kennedy

For Writers

Internal Dialogue

Internal dialogue is the voice inside our heads that we can't ignore, even when we want to. We second-guess ourselves, pass judgment on the world around us, and are at our most emotionally vulnerable. And the same needs to be true for our characters.

Internal dialogue is one of the most powerful tools in a fiction writer's arsenal. It's an advantage we have over TV and movie script writers and playwrights. It's also one of the least understood and most often mismanaged elements of the writing craft.

In *Internal Dialogue: A Busy Writer's Guide*, you'll learn...

- the difference between internal dialogue and narration,
- best practices for formatting internal dialogue,
- ways to use internal dialogue to advance your story,
- how to balance internal dialogue with external action,
- clues to help you decide whether you're overusing or underusing internal dialogue,

- tips for dealing with questions in your internal dialogue,
- and much more!

Showing and Telling in Fiction

You've heard the advice "show, don't tell" until you can't stand to hear it anymore. Yet fiction writers of all levels still seem to struggle with it.

There are three reasons for this. The first is that this isn't an absolute rule. Telling isn't always wrong. The second is that we lack a clear way of understanding the difference between showing and telling. The third is that we're told "show, don't tell," but we're often left without practical ways to know how and when to do that, and how and when not to. So that's what this book is about.

Chapter One defines showing and telling and explains why showing is normally better.

Chapter Two gives you eight practical ways to find telling that needs to be changed to showing and guides you in understanding how to make those changes.

Chapter Three explains how telling can function as a useful first-draft tool.

Chapter Four goes in-depth on the seven situations when telling might be a better choice than showing.

Chapter Five provides you with practical editing tips to help you take what you've learned to the pages of your current novel or short story.

Showing and Telling in Fiction: A Busy Writer's Guide also includes three appendices covering how to use *The Emotion Thesaurus*, dissecting an example so you can see the concepts of showing vs. telling in action, and explaining the closely related topic of As-You-Know-Bob Syndrome.

Dialogue

How do you properly format dialogue? How can you write dialogue unique to each of your characters? Is it okay to start a chapter with dialogue? Writers all agree that great dialogue helps make great fiction, but it's not as easy to write as it looks.

In *Dialogue: A Busy Writer's Guide*, you'll learn

- how to format your dialogue,
- how to add variety to your dialogue so it's not always "on the nose,"
- when you should use dialogue and when you shouldn't,
- how to convey information through dialogue without falling prey to As-You-Know-Bob Syndrome,
- how to write dialogue unique to each of your characters,
- how to add tension to your dialogue,
- whether it's ever okay to start a chapter with dialogue,
- ways to handle contractions (or a lack thereof) in science fiction, fantasy, and historical fiction,
- tricks for handling dialect,
- and much more!

Grammar for Fiction Writers

Not your same old boring grammar guide! This book is fun, fast, and focused on writing amazing fiction.

The world of grammar is huge, but fiction writers don't need to know all the nuances to write well. In fact, some of the rules you were taught in English class will actually hurt your fiction writing, not help it.

Grammar for Fiction Writers won't teach you things you don't need to know. It's all about the grammar that's relevant to you as you write your novels and short stories.

Here's what you'll find inside:

- **Punctuation Basics** including the special uses of dashes and ellipses in fiction, common comma problems, how to format your dialogue, and untangling possessives and contractions.

- **Knowing What Your Words Mean and What They Don't** including commonly confused words, imaginary words and phrases, how to catch and strengthen weak words, and using connotation and denotation to add powerful subtext to your writing.

- **Grammar Rules Every Writer Needs to Know and Follow** such as maintaining an active voice and making the best use of all the tenses for fast-paced writing that feels immediate and draws the reader in.

- **Special Challenges for Fiction Writers** like reversing cause and effect, characters who are unintentionally doing the impossible, and orphaned dialogue and pronouns.

- **Grammar "Rules" You Can Safely Ignore When Writing Fiction**

Twitter for Authors

Building a thriving social media platform doesn't have to steal all your precious writing time or cut into your time with your family. *Twitter for Authors: A Busy Writer's Guide* is about building a successful Twitter platform that's sustainable for busy people.

Twitter often gets a bad reputation from people who don't understand it or don't know how to use it to its full potential to build an author platform. When used correctly, Twitter can be one of the best tools for increasing traffic to your blog and gaining new readers for your books. And it's fun!

In *Twitter for Authors*, you'll learn...

- essential Twitter terminology,
- how to set up your account,
- the differences between TweetDeck and Hootsuite,
- techniques for staying safe on Twitter,
- how to build columns and lists and use them to find readers,
- the value of link shorteners and hashtags,
- what to tweet about,
- the most common mistakes writers make on Twitter,
- how to run a successful Twitter event,
- how to manage your social media time,
- and much more!

Twitter for Authors contains helpful advice for both Twitter newbies and long-time Twitter users who want to take their platform to the next level.

Fiction

Frozen: Two Suspenseful Short Stories

Twisted sleepwalking.

A frozen goldfish in a plastic bag.

And a woman afraid she's losing her grip on reality.

"A Purple Elephant" is a suspense short story about grief and betrayal.

In "The Replacements," a prodigal returns home to find that her parents have started a new family, one with no room for her. This disturbing suspense short story is about the lengths to which we'll go to feel like we're wanted, and how we don't always see things the way they really are.

ABOUT THE AUTHOR

Marcy Kennedy is a science fiction, fantasy, and suspense author, freelance editor, and writing instructor who believes there's always hope. Sometimes you just have to dig a little harder to find it. In a world that can be dark and brutal and unfair, hope is one of our most powerful weapons.

She writes novels that encourage people to keep fighting. She wants to let them know that no one is beyond redemption and that, in the end, good always wins.

She writes books for writers to give them the courage to keep writing. She wants to let them know that they can achieve their dream of creating fantastic stories if they're willing to work for it.

She's also a proud Canadian and the proud wife of a former U.S. Marine; owns four cats, two birds, and a dog who weighs as much as she does; and plays board games and the flute (not at the same time). Sadly, she's also addicted to coffee and jelly beans.

You can find her blogging at www.marcykennedy.com about writing and about the place where real life meets science fiction, fantasy, and myth. To sign up for her new-release mailing list, please go to the link below. Not only will you hear about new releases before anyone else, but you'll also receive exclusive discounts and freebies. Your email address will never be shared, and you can unsubscribe at any time.

Newsletter: http://eepurl.com/Bk2Or

Website: www.marcykennedy.com

Email: marcykennedy@gmail.com

Facebook: www.facebook.com/MarcyKennedyAuthor

Printed in Great Britain
by Amazon